MOSCOW DIARY

Walter Benjamin

Moscow Diary

EDITED BY GARY SMITH
TRANSLATED BY RICHARD SIEBURTH

Harvard University Press
Cambridge, Massachusetts
and London, England
1986

This book first appeared as Issue 35 of *October*, published by
The MIT Press, Cambridge, Massachusetts, in 1986, and is
reprinted by arrangement with the Massachusetts Institute of
Technology. Portions of the book first appeared in German as
Walter Benjamin, *Moskauer Tagebuch*, © Suhrkamp Verlag,
Frankfurt am Main 1980, and are printed here in English by
arrangement with Suhrkamp Verlag.

Library of Congress Cataloging-in-Publication Data

Benjamin, Walter, 1892-1940.
    Moscow diary.

    Translation of: Moskauer Tagebuch.
    Includes bibliographical references and index.
    1. Benjamin, Walter, 1892-1940—Diaries. 2. Benjamin,
Walter, 1892-1940—Journeys—Russian S.F.S.R.—
Moscow. 3. Benjamin, Walter, 1892-1940—Political and
social views. 4. Authors, German—20th century—
Biography. 5. Moscow (R.S.F.S.R.)—
Description. 6. Moscow (R.S.F.S.R.)—Social conditions.
I. Smith, Gary. II. Title.
PT2603.E455Z4713 1986   838'.91203   [B]   86-9964
ISBN 0-674-58743-X
ISBN 0-674-58744-8 (pbk.)

51,866

Contents

MOSCOW DIARY

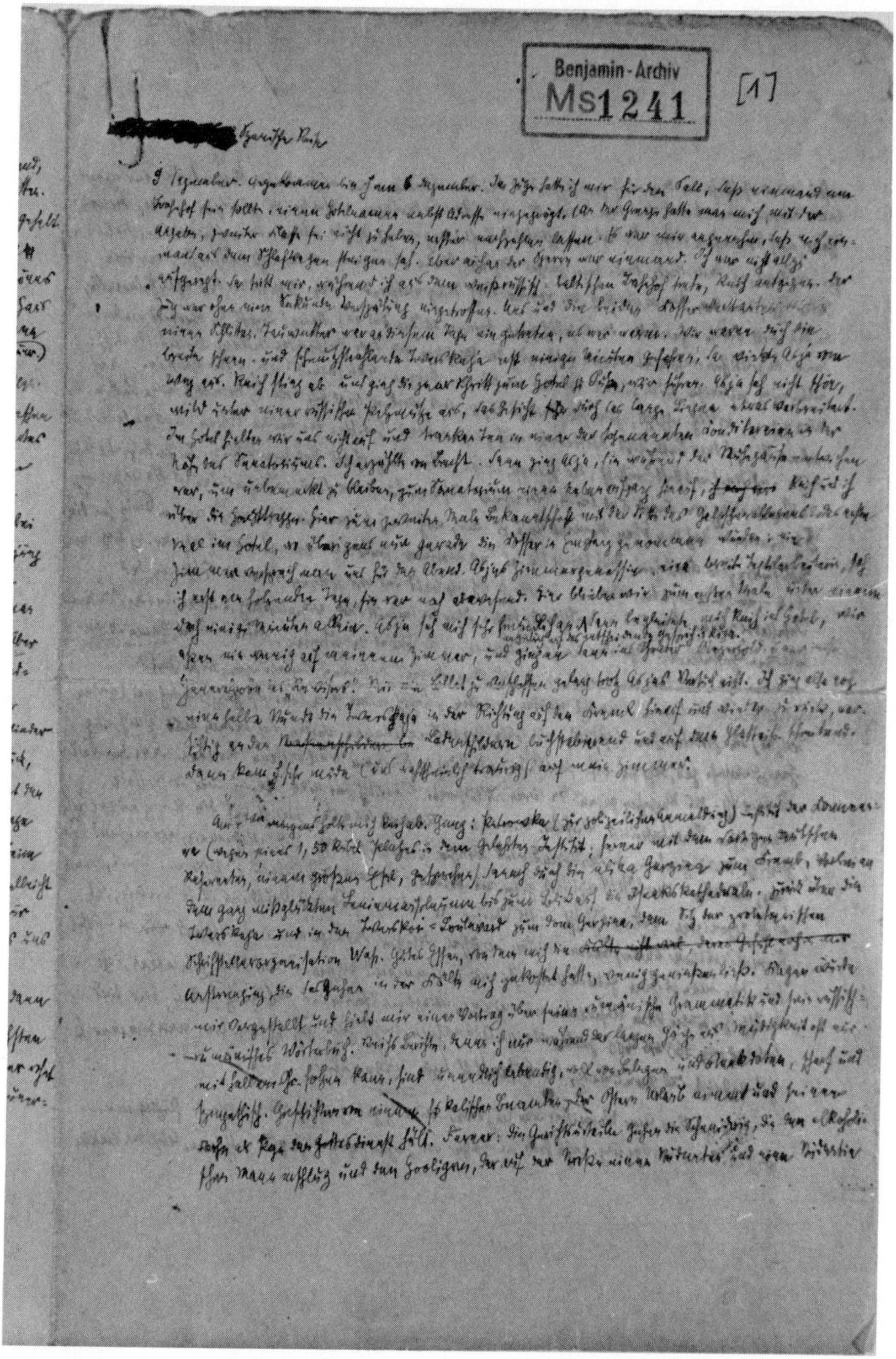

First manuscript page of Benjamin's Moscow Diary.

GERSHOM SCHOLEM

Walter Benjamin's diary dealing with his two-month stay in Moscow from December 6, 1926 to the end of January 1927 is, from what I know of his papers, unique in kind. Absolutely and mercilessly frank, it is without a doubt by far the most personal document that we possess concerning one of the turning points of his life. None of his other surviving attempts at keeping a diary, which inevitably break off after a few pages, can be compared to it, not even the very personal reflections he noted down in 1932 when he was thinking of taking his life.

What we have here is a self-contained piece that deals with a crucial period of his life and that is absolutely free of censorship, which is above all to say: it is free of self-censorship. All of his known personal correspondence that has come down to us tends to adopt a line, one might even call it a partisan tendency, that takes into consideration whomever he is addressing. These letters lack that particular dimension which only emerges from honest, unrestrained self-confrontation and self-assessment. Things are articulated here that were otherwise never explicitly formulated in writing. To be sure, here and there, for example in some of his occasional aphoristic intimations, he hints at these things, but these allusions remain circumspect, "disinfected," having undergone a process of self-censorship. Here, however, they appear in their fully detailed original context, a context of which the few surviving letters he wrote from Moscow — one to me, and one to Jula Radt — give absolutely no indication.

Three factors contributed to Benjamin's journey to Moscow. First of all, his passion for Asja Lacis, and second, his desire to get a closer look at the situation in Russia, and perhaps even to establish some sort of official tie with it, thereby resolving the issue of his eventual membership in the German Communist Party, a question he had been weighing for over two years. A further contributing factor was no doubt provided by the literary obligations he had assumed before setting out on his journey and which committed him to writing an account of the city and its inhabitants, in short, to rendering the "physiognomy" of Moscow. After all, he had partially financed his trip by various advances he had received for pieces related to this journey which he had agreed to submit later. Four publications in early 1927 are the direct outgrowth of these agreements, in particular the long essay "Moscow," which he had discussed with Buber and which appeared in the latter's journal *Die Kreatur*. This essay is a reworking, and often a considerable one at that, of the initial notations contained in the diary. What is astounding about the latter is their unbelievable precision, an unusually intense blend of observation and imagination.

A large portion of the diary is given over to the lively description of his, in the end, futile attempts to establish a productive relationship with various representatives of the literary and artistic life as well as with the officials who concerned themselves with this. He failed in his intent to consolidate these contacts into a position as a correspondent on German literature and culture for Russian publications. This is paralleled by his deliberations, noted down in detail solely here, as to whether or not he should join the German Communist Party; the pros and cons of the matter would eventually lead him to decide against it. He clearly recognized the boundaries beyond which he was unwilling to step.

There is a sharp contrast between the optimistic expectations that Benjamin initially harbored concerning the shape his relations with the Moscow literary milieu might take and the bitter disappointments that awaited him there in reality. His optimism is clearly evident in the previously unpublished letter that he wrote to me on December 10, 1926, only four days after his arrival, and that I have made available for this volume—the only letter, moreover, that he ever wrote to me from Moscow. What eventually became of all his expectations we now learn in painstaking detail from his diary. Little by little, but no less demoralizing because the process was gradual, he lost all his illusions.

Benjamin's own assessment of his experiences in Moscow can be very precisely inferred from a letter he wrote to Martin Buber only three weeks after his return (on February 23, 1927), and in which he announces the imminent completion of his "Moscow" essay. It seems to me that Benjamin's summary deserves to be excerpted and quoted here: "My presentation will be devoid of all theory. In this fashion I hope to succeed in allowing the creatural to speak for itself: inasmuch as I have succeeded in seizing and rendering this very new and disorienting language that echoes loudly through the resounding mask of an environment that has been totally transformed. I want to write a description of Moscow at the present moment in which 'all factuality is already theory' and which would thereby refrain from any deductive abstraction, from any prognostication, and even within certain limits from any judgment—all of which, I am absolutely convinced, cannot be formulated in this case on the basis of spiritual 'data' but only on the basis of economic facts of which few people, even in Russia, have a sufficiently broad grasp. Moscow as it appears at the present reveals a full range of possibilities in schematic form: above all, the possibility that the Revolution might fail or succeed. In either case, something unforeseeable will result and its picture will be far different from any programmatic sketch one might draw of the future. The outlines of this are at present brutally and distinctly visible among the people and their environment."

For the current reader this is accompanied by the heightened realization of a fact that is merely addressed embryonically in the diary, namely that nearly all the individuals with whom he managed to establish contact (all Jewish, almost without exception, whether or not he was aware of it) belonged to the political or artistic opposition — it was still possible more or less to distinguish the two back then. To the extent that I have been able to trace their fates, sooner or later, be it as Trotskyites or under other labels, they would all become victims of Stalin's rule as it began to consolidate its power. Even his friend Asja Lacis would be later forced to spend many years in a camp in the wake of Stalin's "purges." In addition, Benjamin's growing awareness of the opportunism of many of his closest acquaintances, dictated either by fear or by cynicism, was something he could not ignore and in the end led to violent confrontations, even with Asja Lacis.

Benjamin's rather tense relationship with Bernhard Reich, a very intelligent director (formerly with the Deutsches Theater in Berlin) and companion of Asja Lacis (whom he would marry in her later years), was more important to his activities in Moscow and intellectually more instructive than was his relationship with Asja Lacis, who, as the diary makes clear, simply did not have access to as many contacts as Reich did. But even with Reich things were already reaching the breaking point by January 1927 — a profound falling out that is masked only at great pains.

But the heart of the diary is without a doubt what emerges as the infinitely problematic relationship with Asja Lacis (1891–1979). Several years ago she published a book of memoirs, *Professional Revolutionary*, which devotes a chapter to Walter Benjamin. For the reader of that chapter this diary will come as an unpleasant and depressing surprise.

Benjamin first met Asja Lacis in May 1924 on Capri. In the letters he wrote to me from Capri he alluded to her, without ever mentioning her by name, as a "Bolshevik Latvian from Riga," and in reference to a "penetrating insight into the pressing need for radical communism," he characterized her as a "Russian revolutionary from Riga, one of the most remarkable women I have ever met." She was undoubtedly a decisive influence on his life from this point until 1930, at the least. They were together in Berlin in 1924 and in Riga in 1925 and perhaps again in Berlin on one more occasion before he set off for Moscow primarily in order to see her. She was, after Dora Kellner and Jula Cohn [-Radt], the third woman in his life who was of central importance. His erotic attraction to her was linked to the powerful intellectual influence that she exercised over him, to judge from the dedication of his book, *One-Way Street*: "This street is named Asja Lacis Street, after the engineer who laid it through the author." But the diary leaves us without insight into or understanding of precisely this intellectual dimension of the woman he loved. As a narrative of a courtship that remains frustrated almost to the very end of his stay, the diary is desperate in its outright urgency. Admittedly, Asja is sick and hospitalized in a sanatorium from the time he arrives until shortly before his departure, but we learn nothing about the nature of her ailment. The time they spend together is thus for the most part restricted to her room, only on a few occasions does she come to visit him in his hotel. Her daughter, the child of a previous relationship and about eight or nine years old in my estimation, is also in ill health and has been placed in a children's clinic on the outskirts of Moscow. Asja Lacis therefore withdraws from any active participation in his endeavors. She functions merely as a friendly ear for his accounts of his activities, as the almost always elusive object of his courtship, and finally and not exactly infrequently, as his adversary in hostile, wrenching disputes. The times he waits in vain for Asja, her continual rejections, and finally even the erotic cynicism that she displays to no uncertain extent — all this, registered in the diary in desperate detail, makes the absence of any convincing evocation of her intellectual profile doubly enigmatic. This is borne out by everybody who witnessed Benjamin together with Asja Lacis: in conveying their impressions to me, they were all bewildered by these two lovers who did nothing but quarrel. And this was in 1929 and 1930, when she came to Berlin and Frankfurt and Benjamin was getting divorced on her account! Part of the puzzle therefore remains unsolved, which is in fact entirely appropriate to a life such as Walter Benjamin's.

Jerusalem, February 1, 1980

WALTER BENJAMIN

December 9. I arrived December 6th. In the train I had made a mental note of the name and address of a hotel in case there should be nobody waiting for me at the station. (At the border they had made me pay extra to travel first class, claiming there were no more seats in second.) I was relieved that there was no one there to see me emerge from the sleeping car. But there was no one at the platform gate either. I was not overly upset. Then, as I was making my way out of the Belorussian-Baltic railway station, Reich appeared.[2] The train had arrived on time, not a second late. We loaded ourselves and the two suitcases into a sleigh. A thaw had set in that day, it was warm. We had only been under-way a few minutes, driving down the broad Tverskaia with its gleam of snow and mud, when Asja[3] waved to us from the side of the street. Reich got out and walked the short remaining distance to the hotel, we took the sleigh. Asja did not look beautiful, wild beneath her Russian fur hat, her face somewhat puffy from all the time she had spent bedridden. We stopped off briefly at the hotel and then had tea in a so-called pastry shop near the sanatorium.[4] I filled her in about Brecht.[5] Then Asja, who had slipped away during a rest period,

1.   Benjamin obliterated the initial title of his manuscript, *Moscow Diary*, and wrote *Spanish Journey* beside it. It is unclear whether this subsequent title (which may have been added years later) was added for reasons of political or personal safety, or whether it may have been intended as a metaphorical characterization of his Moscow experiences or as a private literary allusion.
2.   Bernhard Reich (1894–1972), playwright, director, and critic, was the lifelong companion of Asja Lacis. Originally Austrian, he became a Soviet citizen in the mid-1920s. He wrote a monograph, *Brecht*, in Russian (Moscow, 1960) and published his reminiscences as *Im Wettlauf mit der Zeit: Erinnerungen aus fünf Jahrzehnten deutscher Theatergeschichte*, Berlin, Henschelverlag, 1970; this book appeared in Russian as *V'ena Berlin Moskva Berlin*, Moscow, Iskusstvo, 1972.
3.   Asja Lacis (1891–1979), Latvian actress and theater director, whom Benjamin first met in Capri during the summer of 1924. She published recollections of Benjamin, Meyerhold, and Brecht in *Revolutionär im Beruf*, H. Brenner, ed., Munich, Rogner and Bernhard, 1972. After publishing a book on German theater (*Revolutsii teatr germani*, Moscow, Goslitizdat, 1935), she was interned for roughly fifteen years until after Stalin's death. A bibliography of her publications is appended to M. Miglane, et. al., *Anna Lacis*, Riga, Liesma, 1973, pp. 250–255.
4.   In the wake of a nervous breakdown in September 1926, Lacis was living at the Rott sanatorium near Gorky Street.
5.   According to Lacis's autobiography, Benjamin met Brecht in Berlin before his Moscow

took a side entrance back into the sanatorium in order to escape notice while Reich and I went in by the main stairs. Here, for the second time, encountered the custom of removing one's galoshes. The first time had been at the hotel, even though it involved no more than checking in the luggage; they had promised us a room that night. Asja's roommate, a hefty textile worker, was absent, I would see her for the first time the following day. Here we were, alone together for the first time under the same roof for a few minutes. Asja was looking at me very affectionately. An allusion to the decisive conversation in Riga. Then Reich accompanied me back to the hotel, we had a bite in my room, and went to the Meyerhold Theater.[6] It was the first dress rehearsal for *The Inspector General*.[7] I was unable to get a ticket despite Asja's efforts on my behalf. So I strolled up Tverskaia in the direction of the Kremlin for half an hour and came back, carefully spelling out the shop signs, carefully proceeding over the ice. Then, very tired (and, very likely, sad), I returned to my room.

On the morning of the 7th, Reich came to fetch me. Itinerary: Petrovka (to register with the police), the Kameneva Institute[8] (for a 1.50 ruble seat at the Institute of Culture; talked, moreover, with their local German representative, an utter ass), then via Herzen Street to the Kremlin, passing in front of the totally botched Lenin mausoleum and then on to the scenic view of the St. Isaac Cathedral. Return via Tverskaia, following Tverskoi Boulevard to Dom Herzena,[9] the headquarters of the Organization of Proletarian Writers, VAPP.[10] A good meal, which I barely appreciated, given the exertion which the walk in the cold had involved. Kogan[11] was introduced to me and expounded on his Rumanian grammar and his Russian-Rumanian dictionary. The tales Reich tells, which in the course of our long walks I am often too tired to listen to with both ears, are endlessly vivacious, filled with anecdotes and specifics,

journey; most scholars, however, place their first meeting (arranged by Lacis) in Berlin in May 1929. See Rolf Tiedemann, *Dialektik im Stillstand*, Frankfurt, Suhrkamp, 1983, p. 45; and Klaus Völker, *Brecht Chronicle*, New York, Continuum, 1975, p. 54.
6.   Vsevolod Emilevich Meyerhold (1874–1942) was given his own theater in 1923, the Teatr imeni Meyerholda (TIM).
7.   The rehearsals for Meyerhold's production of Gogol's *The Inspector General* lasted one and a half years. In contrast to the first half of the 1920s, when he staged a large number of plays, often simultaneously, over a short period of time, Meyerhold was diverted from his preparation of this production only briefly, to rectify the direction of *Roar, China!*. See note 91.
8.   Another name for VOKS—Vsesoiuznoe obshchestvo kulturnoi sviazi s zagranitse (Federal Society for Foreign Cultural Relations), 1925–1958. Its director from 1925–1929 was Olga Kameneva (1883–1941), the sister of Trotsky.
9.   Herzen House, named after the writer Alexandr Herzen (1812–1870), served as one of the meeting places of VAPP during this period.
10.   Acronym of the Vserossiiskaia assotsiastsiia proletarskikh pissatelei (Federal Association of Proletarian Writers), founded 1920.
11.   Petr Semenovich Kogan (1872–1932), critic and literary historian, professor of Romance and Germanic Philology at the universities of St. Petersburg and Moscow, president of the Academy of Arts since its inception in 1921.

sharp and amusing. Stories about a bureaucrat who works for the Treasury Department, and goes on vacation at Easter and celebrates mass as a pope. And then: the one about the conviction of a seamstress who struck her alcoholic husband dead, and the hooligan who attacked a male and female student on the street. And then: the one about Stanislavsky's staging of a white-guard play:[12] how it was initially submitted to the board of censors, only one of them taking notice of it and returning it, recommending certain modifications. Then months later, having made the necessary modifications, the play is finally performed for the censors. Banned. Stanislavsky to Stalin: I'm ruined, all my capital was tied up in that play. Stalin deciding: "the play is not dangerous." It premieres, protested by the communists, who are kept at a distance by the militia. Then the story about the novella à clef dealing with the Frunze case,[13] which supposedly was carried out against his wishes and on Stalin's orders . . . then the political news: members of the opposition removed from important positions. And in identical fashion: countless Jews removed from middle-level posts. Anti-Semitism in the Ukraine. — After VAPP, utterly exhausted, I proceed on to Asja's on my own. A crowd soon gathers. A Latvian woman arrives and sits down on the bed next to her, then Chestakov[14] and his wife, and between these two, on the one hand, and Asja and Reich on the other, a violent argument breaks out in Russian about Meyerhold's production of *The Inspector General*. The major point of contention is his use of velvet and silk, fourteen costumes for his wife;[15] the performance, moreover, lasts five and a half hours. After the meal, Asja comes to my room; Reich is also present. Before leaving, Asja tells the story of her illness. Reich accompanies her back to the sanatorium, and then returns. I'm lying in bed — he wants to work. But he soon interrupts himself and we talk about the situation of intellectuals here and in Germany; and about the techniques of contemporary writing in both countries. Which leads into Reich's reservations about joining the Party. He focuses on the Party's reactionary bent in cultural matters. The leftist movements which had proved useful during the period of wartime communism are now being completely discarded. It's only quite recently that the proletarian writers have been officially recognized as such (despite Trotsky), although they were at the same time made to understand that they could in no event count on governmental sup-

12. I.e., *Dni Turbinych* (*The Days of the Turbins*), adapted for the stage by Konstantin Stanislavsky (1863–1938) from the novel *The White Guard* (1924) by Mikhail Bulgakov (1891–1940).
13. Mikhail V. Frunze (1885–1925), a general and leading Party official; later Minister of War and the Navy. Benjamin is referring to Boris Pil'nyak's *A Tale of the Unextinguished Moon*, published in the fifth issue of *Novyi Mir* (New World) in 1926.
14. Viktor A. Chestakov (1898–1957) was the chief stage designer for the Theater of the Revolution from 1922–1927, then with the Meyerhold Theater until its closing in 1937.
15. Zinaida Raikh (1894–1939) frequently played the leading roles in Meyerhold's productions. Some of the harshest criticism of Meyerhold's production was directed at the allegedly "inflated" role of his wife; see, for example, Viktor Shklovsky's "Fifteen Portions of the Mayor's Wife," in the *Krasnaia gazeta* of December 22, 1926.

port. Then the Lelevich case[16] — measures taken against the cultural front of the left. Lelevich had composed a treatise on the methods of Marxist literary criticism. — In Russia, they put the utmost weight on taking an extremely nuanced political position. In Germany, a vague and general political background suffices, though it [would] nonetheless be essential to demand the same thing there. — The method of writing in Russia: the broad exposition of an argument and, if possible, nothing further. The cultural level of the public is so low that formulations would inevitably remain incomprehensible. By contrast, in Germany the only thing demanded is: results. No one cares to know how you have arrived at them. Which explains why German newspapers only place a minimal amount of space at the disposition of their reporters; here, articles of 500 to 600 lines are not a rarity. This discussion went on for a long while. My room is well heated and spacious, a pleasant place to stay.

December 8. Asja dropped by in the morning. I gave her presents, hastily showed her my book with the dedication.[17] I also showed (and gave) her the dust jacket Stone had designed.[18] It pleased her a great deal. Then Reich arrived. Later I went to the state bank with him to change money. There we talked briefly with Neumann's father. December 10. Then via a newly constructed arcade to Petrovka. There is a display of porcelain wares in the arcade. But Reich just keeps on walking. In the street where the Hotel Liverpool is I see the pastry shops for the second time. (I here insert the story of Toller's Moscow visit,[19] which I heard about my first day. He was welcomed with unbelievable pomp. Throughout the city posters proclaim his arrival. He is given a staff of assistants, translators, secretaries, beautiful women. Lectures by him are announced. There is, however, a session of the Comintern taking place in Moscow at the same time. Werner,[20] the archenemy of Toller, is among the German delegates.

16.   Grigory Lelevich (1901–1945), pseudonym of Labori Gilelevich Kalmanson, poet, critic, and one of the editors of the magazine *Na postu* (*On Guard*), which published six issues, 1923–1926. He cofounded a group of the same name in 1923 but lost his influence over it in 1926 as a result of internal power struggles. Expelled from the Party, he died in a camp in 1945.
17.   *Einbahnstrasse*, Berlin, Rowohlt, 1928. Selections from *One-Way Street* may be found in Edmund Jephcott's translation in *Reflections*, Peter Demetz, ed., New York, Harcourt, Brace, Jovanovich, 1978. Benjamin's dedication to Lacis reads: "This street is named Asja Lacis Street, after the engineer who laid it through the author."
18.   Sascha Stone (d. 1939?), Russian-born fashion and advertising photographer well-known in Berlin during the 1920s. Stone studied sculpture and drawing in Paris, then established a photography studio in Berlin; in 1933 he fled to Belgium. He contributed the photomontage on the dustjacket of the first edition of *One-Way Street*; he also photographed Jula Radt's sculpted head of Benjamin.
19.   Ernst Toller (1893–1939), leading figure in the short-lived Bavarian Soviet Republic of 1919. His plays were often performed on the Soviet stage during the 1920s. He was in Moscow from March to May, 1926. See Toller, *Quer durch*, Berlin, G. Kiepenheur, 1930.
20.   Paul Werner, pseudonym of Paul Frölich (1884–1953). He published an attack on Toller in *Pravda* on March 20, 1926; Toller replied six days later in a letter to the editor.

Sascha Stone. Jacket design for Walter Benjamin's
One-Way Street.

He requests or writes an article in *Pravda*: Toller has betrayed the Revolution,
is responsible for the collapse of one of the German Soviet Republics. *Pravda*
adds a short editorial note: Our apologies, we were unaware. Whereupon Toller
becomes persona non grata in Moscow. He arrives at the auditorium where he
is to deliver a much-publicized lecture — the building is closed. The Kameneva
Institute informs him: Our apologies, the hall was unavailable. (Someone had
forgotten to telephone him.) Back at VAPP at noon. A bottle of mineral water
costs one ruble. Afterward, Reich and I go visit Asja. To soothe her spirits
Reich arranges, much against her will and mine, a game of dominos between
us in the recreation room of the sanatorium. Sitting next to her, I feel like I'm
some character out of a novel by Jacobsen.[21] Reich is playing chess with a famous old communist, a man who lost his eye in the war or in the civil war, and
who is completely wrecked and wrung out like so many of the old-time communists who are not already dead. Asja and I have barely returned to her room
when Reich comes by to escort me to Granovsky's.[22] Asja accompanies us down

21. Probably the Danish novelist Jens Peter Jacobsen (1847–1885).
22. Alexandr Granovsky (1890–1935), director of the Jewish Academic Theater of Moscow. A

Tverskaia for a bit. I buy her some halvah in a pastry shop and she turns back. Granovsky is a Latvian Jew from Riga. He has created a farcical, anti-religious, and, from outward appearances, fairly anti-Semitic form of satirical comedy, a parody of slang operettas. His mannerisms are decidedly Western, he is somewhat sceptical about bolshevism and the discussion revolves primarily around theater and money matters. The talk turns to housing. The price of apartments here is calculated by the square meter. The cost per square meter is proportional to the salary of the tenant. In addition, the rental and heating fee is tripled for anything that exceeds the thirteen square meters allocated per person. We had not been expected, so instead of a full meal there was an improvised cold dinner. A discussion in my room with Reich about the *Encyclopedia*.[23]

December 9. Asja again came by in the morning. I gave her a few things, then we went out for a walk. Asja spoke of me. We turned back at the Liverpool. I then went home; Reich was already there. We each worked for an hour — I on writing the Goethe article. Then to the Kameneva Institute to work out a reduced hotel rate for me. And then on to a meal. This time not at VAPP. The fare was outstanding, particularly the red cabbage soup. And then on to the Liverpool and its amiable owner, a Latvian. It was twelve degrees [centigrade]. I was fairly exhausted after lunch and could not go to Lelevich's on foot as I had intended. We had to be driven a short way. Then one passes through a large garden or park area, scattered with housing complexes. All the way to the rear, a lovely black and white wooden house with Lelevich's apartment on the second floor. As we enter the house we meet Bezymensky,[24] who is just leaving. A steep wooden staircase and, immediately behind a door, the kitchen with an open fire. And then a rudimentary vestibule where a number of coats are hanging, then across a room apparently containing alcoves, and into Lelevich's study. His appearance is quite difficult to describe. Fairly tall, wearing a blue Russian tunic, he makes few movements (moreover, the small room filled with people, pins him to the chair at his desk). The most curious thing is his long, apparently unarticulated face with its broad planes. His chin is far longer than any I have ever seen, except for the one on the invalid Grommer,[25] and it is barely cleft.

brief 1928 note on Granovsky may be found in Walter Benjamin, *Gesammelte Schriften* (henceforth *GS*), Rolf Tiedemann and Hermann Schweppenhäuser, eds., Frankfurt, Suhrkamp, 1972–1977, IV, pp. 518–522.

23.   Before leaving for Moscow, Benjamin had been invited (probably on Reich's recommendation) to write an article on Goethe for the *Bolshaia sovetskaia entsiklopediia* (*Great Soviet Encyclopedia*).

24.   Alexandr Ilich Bezymensky (1898–1973), poet and activist; in 1926 he belonged to the same literary faction within VAPP as did Lelevich.

25.   Jakob Grommer (1879–1933), Russian, studied mathematics in Germany and worked as Albert Einstein's assistant for ten years, longer than any of Einstein's other collaborators. His extreme facial disfigurement was caused by acromegaly.

He appears to be very calm, but one senses in him the gnawing silence of the fanatic. He asks Reich a number of questions concerning me. On the opposite side of the room, there are two people sitting on the bed, the one in the black tunic is young and quite handsome. Only members of the literary opposition are gathered here to be with him during the final hour before his departure. He is being transferred. Initially he had been ordered to Novosibirsk. "What you need," they had told him, "is not a town with its inevitably limited sphere of action, but rather an entire administrative region." He was able, however, to prevent this and now they are sending him, "at the disposal of the Party," to Saratov, twenty-four hours from Moscow, without his yet knowing whether he is going to be employed there as an editor, as a salesman for a state production cooperative, or whatever. His wife spends most of the time in the next room receiving additional visitors — she is a creature whose expression is highly energetic and yet harmonious, small, a typical southern Russian. She will accompany him for the first three days. Lelevich has a fanatic's optimism: he bemoans the fact that tomorrow he will not be able to hear Trotsky's speech to the Comintern on behalf of Zinoviev, and claims the Party is on the verge of a turnabout.[26] As we say goodbye in the hallway, I ask Reich to convey a few friendly words on my part. Then we go to Asja's. Maybe it was only then that the domino game took place. In the evening, both Reich and Asja intended to drop by my place. But only Asja came. I gave her presents: blouse, hose. We talk. I observe that she basically forgets nothing that involves us. (That afternoon she had told me she thought that I was doing well. That it was not true that I was going through a crisis.) Before she leaves, I read her the section about wrinkles in *One-Way Street*.[27] Then I help her into her galoshes. I was already asleep when Reich came by around midnight with some reassuring news he wanted me to convey to Asja the following morning. He had made preparations to move out of his lodgings. He is sharing quarters with a madman, which considerably complicates the already difficult question of living arrangements.

26. Leon Trotsky (1879–1940), Grigory Zinoviev (1883–1936), and Lev Kamenev (1883–1936) were at this point leaders of the opposition against Stalin. Trotsky was banished in 1929.

27. The passage (in Edmund Jephcott's translation) runs as follows: "He who loves is attached not only to the 'faults' of the beloved, not only to the whims and weakness of a woman. Wrinkles in the face, moles, shabby clothes, and a lopsided walk bind him more lastingly and relentlessly than any beauty. This has long been known. And why? If the theory is correct that feeling is not located in the head, that we sentiently experience a window, a cloud, a tree not in our brains but, rather, in the place where we see it, then we are, in looking at our beloved, too, outside ourselves. But in a torment of tension and ravishment. Our feeling, dazzled, flutters like a flock of birds in the woman's radiance. And as birds seek refuge in the leafy recesses of a tree, feelings escape into the shaded wrinkles, the awkward movements and inconspicuous blemishes of the body we love, where they can lie low in safety. And no passer-by would guess that it is just here, in what is defective and censurable, that the fleeting darts of adoration nestle" (*Reflections*, p. 68).

December 10. We go see Asja in the morning. Since morning visits are prohibited, we talk to her in the lobby for a minute. She is [tired] after the carbonic acid bath which she has taken for the first time and which has done her a great deal of good. Then to the Kameneva Institute. The document I need to get a reduced rate at the hotel was supposed to be ready, but is not. On the other hand, the opportunity for an extremely wide-ranging discussion of theater questions with the unoccupied gentleman and the young lady in the anteroom. I am to be received by Kameneva herself the following day and arrangements are being made to find me theater tickets for tonight. Unfortunately there are none available for the operetta theater. Reich drops me off at VAPP; I spend two and a half hours there with my Russian grammar; then he returns with Kogan for lunch. In the afternoon I see Asja only briefly. She had had an argument with Reich about living arrangements and sends me away. I read Proust in my room while eating marzipan. I go to the sanatorium in the evening and at the entrance I meet Reich, who had just stepped out for some cigarettes. We wait a few minutes in the hallway, and then Asja appears. Reich puts us on the tram and we ride to the music studio.[28] We are received by its administrator. He displays to us a letter of congratulations, in French, from Casella,[29] ushers us around all the rooms (the lobby is already filling with people well before curtain time, they come directly to the theater from their places of work), and shows us the concert hall. An extraordinarily loud, rather ugly carpet occupies the lobby. Probably an expensive Aubusson. The walls are hung with authentic old paintings (one of which is unframed). Here, just as in the official reception chamber of the Institute for International Cultural Relations, one notices the extremely valuable pieces of furniture. We have seats in the second row. Rimsky-Korsakov's *The Czar's Bride* is to be performed — the first opera that Stanislavsky has recently staged.[30] A discussion concerning Toller, how Asja had escorted him, how he wanted to give her something as a gift, how she had picked out the most inexpensive belt for herself, and the crazy remarks he made. We make our way to the lobby during one of the breaks. But there are three of them. They are far too long and tire Asja out. Conversation about the ochre-yellow Italian scarf she is wearing. I explain to her that she feels uneasy in my presence. During the final entr'acte, the administrator approaches us. Asja speaks with him. He invites me to the next new production (*Eugene Onegin*).[31] At the end, difficulties recouping our coats. Two theater employees cordon off the middle of the stair-

28.   The Musical Studio of the Moskovskii Khudozhestvennyi Teatr (Moscow Art Theater), or MKHAT, shared the Dmitrovsky Theater building with Stanislavsky's State Opera Studio.
29.   Benjamin is probably referring to F. D. Ostrogradsky, since it is unlikely that he means Stanislavsky. Alfredo Casella (1883–1947), Italian composer and musician.
30.   *The Czar's Bride* opened on November 28, 1926; it marked the turn of Stanislavsky's attention to classic Russian operas in the Opera Theater.
31.   In fact, Tschaikovsky's *Eugene Onegin* had already been in the Opera Studio's repertoire and was the first complete opera produced by Stanislavsky.

way in order to regulate the flow of the crowd into the tiny cloakrooms. Return the way we came, on a small unheated streetcar with frosted windows.

December 11. Some words on Moscow's characteristics. During my first few days I am above all struck by the difficulty of getting used to walking on the sheet ice of the streets. I have to watch my step so carefully that I cannot look around very much. The situation improved when Asja bought me a pair of galoshes yesterday morning (I'm writing this on the 12th). It was not as difficult as Reich had claimed. The numerous one- and two-story buildings are typical of the city's architecture. They give it the appearance of a summer vacation colony, looking at them one feels doubly cold. The paint jobs are often multicolored, pale in hue: above all red, but also blue, yellow (and, as Reich also says) green. The sidewalk is strikingly narrow, they are as stingy with the ground as they are spendthrift with the airspace. In addition, the ice has formed so thickly along the edges of the houses that a portion of the sidewalk remains unusable. Nor is there any clear demarcation between sidewalk and pavement: the snow and ice

Torgsin store on Petrovka Street.

even out the various levels of the street. One often comes across cordons in front of the state stores: one stands in line for butter and other important staples. There are countless shops and even more merchants whose entire inventory consists of little more than a washbasket of apples, tangerines, or peanuts. In order to protect their produce from the cold, they place it under woolen blankets on top of which two or three specimen items are displayed. A profusion of breads and other baked products: rolls of every size, pretzels, and in the pastry shops, luscious tarts. Fantastic edifices or flowers are constructed out of spun sugar. Yesterday afternoon I was in a pastry shop with Asja. They serve cups of whipped cream there. Asja had a cup with meringue, I had coffee. We sat in the middle of the room, facing each other over a small table. Asja reminded me of my intention to write something critical of psychology, and I once again realized just to what extent the possibility of tackling these subjects depends on my contact with her. At any rate, we were unable to extend our hour in the cafe as we had hoped. I left the sanatorium not at four, but only at five. Reich wanted us to wait for him, he was not sure whether he had a meeting. Finally we got going. We looked at the shopwindows along Petrovka. My attention was drawn by a splendid store featuring articles made out of wood. At my request, Asja bought me a tiny little pipe. I will come back here later to buy toys for Stefan and Daga.[32] They have those Russian eggs, each one encased in another, and animals carved out of lovely soft wood. In another shopwindow there were Russian laces and embroidered cloths whose designs, according to Asja, the peasant women pattern after the frost-flowers on their windows. This was our second walk of the day. Asja had dropped by in the morning, had written to Daga, and then, the weather being beautiful, we took a stroll on Tverskaia. On our way back we stopped in front of a store where there were Christmas candles. Asja commented on them. Later, again to the Kameneva with Reich. I finally receive my hotel reduction. They wanted to send me to see *Cement*[33] in the evening. But Reich later thought a performance at Granovsky's would be a better idea, since Asja wanted to go out to the theater and *Cement* would probably be too unsettling for her. But after all the arrangements had finally been made, Asja was not feeling well enough, so I went on my own, while she and Reich went to my room. There were three one-act plays, the first two were beneath mention, the third one, an assembly of rabbis, a kind of choric comedy set to Jewish melodies, seemed far superior, but I could not follow the action and was so exhausted by my day and by all the breaks in the performance that I fell asleep at various points. — That night Reich slept in my room. — My hair is very electric here.

---

32.   Stefan (1919-1972) was the son of Walter and Dora Benjamin (1890-1964); Daga was Asja Lacis's daughter.
33.   *Cement*, 1925 novel by Fyodor Gladkov (1883–1958). Benjamin's review of the German translation of this novel appeared in June 1927 (*GS*, III, pp. 61–63).

December 12. Reich took a walk with Asja in the morning. Then they dropped in on me — I was still in the process of dressing. Asja sat on the bed. I got a great deal of pleasure out of the way she was unpacking my suitcases and tidying up my things; in the process she picked out two ties for herself that she liked. Then she recounted how she used to devour trashy serial novels when she was little. She would hide the small booklets from her mother in her schoolbooks, but one day she had acquired a large bound volume of *Laura* and it came into the hands of her mother. On another occasion, she ran out of the house in the middle of the night in order to get the next installment of a dime novel from one of her girlfriends. The latter's father was at an utter loss when he answered the door — he wanted to know what she was doing there, and realizing the mess she had gotten herself into, she replied that she herself hadn't the faintest idea. — Lunch with Reich in a small cellar restaurant. The afternoon in the deserted sanatorium was excruciating. With Asja still the usual switching back and forth between the formal *Sie* and the informal *Du.* She was not well. Later we walked down Tverskaia. Then, as we were later sitting in a cafe, Asja and Reich got into a big argument, during which Reich made it clear that he was planning to cut all his ties with Germany and concentrate on Russian matters. Evening spent alone with Reich in my room: I studied the guidebook and he worked on his review of the dress rehearsal of *The Inspector General.* There are no trucks in Moscow, no delivery vans, etc. Whether it be a small purchase or a major shipment, everything has to go by tiny sled or *izvozchik.*

December 13. During the morning I improved my sense of orientation in the city by taking a long walk along the inner boulevards to the central post office and then back across Lubianka Square to Dom Herzena. I solved the mystery of the man with the alphabet board: he was selling letters which one can affix to one's galoshes in order to prevent mix-ups. As I was taking my walk, I was again struck by the number of stores selling Christmas-tree decorations; when I had briefly stepped out with Asja an hour previously, they were also everywhere on Amskaia Tverskaia. The decorations often seem brighter behind the panes of the shopwindow than they do on the tree. As we were walking along Amskaia Tverskaia, we encountered a group of Komsomols[34] marching to music. This music, like that of the Soviet troops, seems to be a combination of whistles and songs. Asja spoke of Reich. She asked me to bring him the latest issue of *Pravda.* In the afternoon at Asja's, Reich read us his preliminary account of Meyerhold's production of *The Inspector General.* It is quite good. While he had (previously) fallen asleep in the chair in Asja's room, I read her selections from *One-Way Street.* During the course of my long morning tour, I also

34. Members of the Kommunisticheskii Soiuz Molodezhi (Komsomol), the Bolshevik youth organization.

noticed something else: market women, peasant women, standing next to their baskets of wares (sometimes also a sled like those they use as children's wagons here in winter). In these baskets lie apples, candies, nuts, sugar figurines, half hidden under cloth. You would think that some sweet grandmother had looked around before leaving her house and had picked out all the things she could take to surprise her grandchild. Having packed them up, she is now standing on the street, taking a short rest on the way. I again saw the Chinese who make artificial flowers out of paper like the ones I brought back to Stefan from Marseilles. But here the paper animals seem more frequently to take the form of exotic deep-sea fish. Then there are the men with baskets full of wooden toys, wagons and spades, the wagons yellow and red, the children's shovels yellow or red. There are others walking around with bundles of colorful weathervanes on their shoulders. The craftsmanship of all this is far more simple and sturdy than in Germany, its peasant origins clearly apparent. I found a woman in a corner selling tree decorations. The glass orbs, yellow and red, glinted in the sun, it was like an enchanted basket of apples, each fruit shot through with different reds and yellows. There is also a more direct relation between wood and color here than elsewhere. One notices it in the crudest of toys as well as in the most sophisticated lacquer work. — Some Mongols stand by the Kitai gorod wall.[35] The winter is probably no less harsh where they come from and their ragged furs are no worse than those of the locals. Still, they are the only people one spontaneously pities on account of the climate. They stand no more than five paces from each other and offer leather briefcases for sale; each one's wares are identical to those of his neighbor. There must be some collusion behind all this, for they can hardly be serious about entering into such futile competition with each other. Here as in Riga the shop signs feature attractive primitive painting. Shoes falling from a basket, a Pomeranian running off with a sandal in his mouth. In front of a Turkish eating place two suspended signs depicting men in fezzes decorated with crescents sitting at their meal. Asja is right to point out that everywhere, even in advertisements, the people characteristically demand that some tangible action be represented. — Evening with Reich at Illés's.[36] Later joined by the director of the Theater of the Revolution,[37] which will premiere Illés's play on December 30th. This director is a former Red Army general who played a decisive part in the annihilation of Vrangel[38] and was twice named in Trotsky's general orders. Later he committed a stupid political blun-

---

35.   An old section of Moscow that includes Red Square and borders on the Kremlin.
36.   Bela Illés (1895–1974), the Hungarian writer, had lived in the Soviet Union since 1923; subsequently he became general secretary of the International Union of Revolutionary Writers (1925–1933) and a general in the Red Army during World War II.
37.   V. S. Starukhin.
38.   Baron Petr Vrangel (1878–1928), Russian general who supported Kornilov's attempt to overthrow the Petrograd soviet. After his defeat by the Red Army in the last major battle of the civil war, he fled abroad.

der which brought his career to a standstill, and since he had earlier been a man of letters, they gave him this position as a theater director which, however, demands little effort. He appears to be fairly dumb. The conversation was not especially lively. In addition, on Reich's recommendation, I was careful about what I said. Plekhanov's theory of art was discussed.[39] The room contains only a few items of furniture, the most noticeable of which are a rickety child's bed and a bathtub. The boy was still up when we arrived, is later put to bed screaming, but does not go to sleep as long as we are there.

December 14 (written on the 15th). I shall not see Asja today. The situation in the sanatorium is growing critical; yesterday evening they let her leave only after protracted negotiations and this morning she did not come to fetch me as previously arranged. We were planning to buy material for her dress. I've only been here a week and already I have to confront the ever-increasing difficulties of seeing her, not to mention of seeing her alone. — Yesterday morning she burst in on me, agitated, more disturbing than disturbed as is so often the case, as if she were terrified of spending a minute in my room. I accompanied her to the offices of a commission to which she had been summoned. Told her what I had learned the previous evening: that Reich had high hopes for a new position as a theater critic for an extremely important publication. We crossed Sadovaia. All in all I said very little, she spoke with great animation about her work with children at the children's center. For the second time I heard the story about the child in her care who had bashed in the skull of another of her children. Curiously enough, it was only now that I understood this rather simple story (which could have had grave consequences for Asja; but the doctors were convinced that the child would be saved). This often happens to me: I barely hear what she is saying because I am examining her so intently. She expanded on her idea: that children must be divided up into groups, because it is utterly impossible to keep the wildest ones — she calls them the most gifted ones — busy with the others. They simply get bored with the things that absorb normal children. And it is very evident that Asja, as she herself says, is most successful with the wildest children. Asja also spoke of the things she was writing, three articles for a Latvian communist newspaper that appears in Moscow: this paper reaches Riga by illegal means and it is very useful for her to be read there.[40] The office of the commission is located at the intersection of Strasnoi Boulevard and Petrovka. I walked back and forth on the latter for half an hour while waiting for her. When she finally emerged, we went to the

39.   The twenty-four volume edition of G. V. Plekhanov's writings, *Sochinenija*, Moscow, 1923–27, was just being completed.
40.   She is referring to either *Jauna Vientba* (*New Unity*) or *Krievijas Ctna* (*Russian News*), two journals to which she contributed during this period.

Gosbank,[41] where I had to change money. I was feeling very energetic that morning and was therefore able to talk to her very calmly and concisely about my Moscow stay and its ever-dwindling prospects. This made an impression on her. She told me that the doctor whose treatment had saved her had expressly forbidden her to remain in the city and had recommended she go to a sanatorium in the woods. She had, however, stayed on, fearing the solitude of the woods and also on my account. We stood in front of a furrier's shop where Asja had already stopped once before during our first walk along Petrovka. A splendid fur outfit with variegated pearls was hanging on the wall. We went in to find out how much it cost and learned that it was a piece of Tungus work (and thus not an "Eskimo" suit as Asja had thought). It was priced at two hundred and fifty rubles. Asja wanted it. I told her: "If I buy it, I'll have to leave right off." But she made me promise that I would some day give her a big present that would remain with her for the rest of her life. One gets to the Gosbank from Petrovka via an arcade which contains a shop where antiques are sold on commission. There was a splendid inlaid Empire armoire in the window. Toward the end of the arcade porcelain was being packed or unpacked near wooden display stands. As we were making our way back to the bus station, a few very good minutes. Then my audience with Kameneva. In the afternoon, I wander through the city: I cannot go visit Asja, Knorin[42] is with her — a very important Latvian communist, a member of the supreme board of censors. (And the same thing today; as I write this, Reich is with her.) My afternoon ends in the French cafe on Stolechnikov in front of a cup of coffee. — As for the city: Byzantine church architecture does not seem to have developed its own style of window. The effect is magical, but somewhat unsettling; drab, secular windows that open onto the street from the spires and assembly halls of the church as if from living rooms. Inside, the orthodox priest living like a bonze in his pagoda. The lower portion of the St. Basil Cathedral could well be the ground floor of a boyar's mansion. But the crosses atop the domes often resemble gigantic earrings attached to the sky. — The luxury that has lodged itself in this ailing, run-down city like tartar in a diseased mouth: the N. Kraft chocolate store, the elegant fashion boutique on Petrovka, with its immense porcelain vases standing among the furs, hideous and frigid. — The begging is not as aggressive as in the South, where the persistency of the ragamuffins still betrays a vestige of vitality. Here it is a corporation of the dying. The street-corners, particularly in those quarters where foreigners do business, are covered with bundles of rags — beds in the great open-air sickbay called Moscow. The begging on streetcars is organized differently. Some of the looplines make

41.   State bank (*Gos*, abbreviation of *gosudarstvennyi*).
42.   Vilis Knorin (1890–1938), high Party and government official, director of the agitprop section of the Party's Central Committee in 1926–1927.

Shot of homeless child from Dziga Vertov's Forward Soviet! *1926.*

long stops along the way. At which point the beggars slip into the car or a child places itself in a corner and begins singing. Then it collects kopeks. One rarely sees anybody give. Begging has lost its most powerful base, the guilty social conscience that opens purses far wider than pity. — Arcades. They contain an utterly indigenous array of tiers and galleries which appear to be as deserted as those of the cathedrals. The bulky felt footwear that peasants and prosperous women march around in makes tight-fitting boots seem like intimate apparel items, as constricting as corsets. *Valenki* [felt boots] are fancy dress for the feet. To return to the churches: most of them are poorly maintained and as cold and empty as the interior of the St. Basil cathedral when I visited it. But the glow that now shines only sporadically from the altars onto the snow has been well preserved in the neighborhood made up of small wooden booths. Their narrow snow-covered alleyways are silent, one hears only the soft patter of the Jewish clothiers whose stall adjoins that of the stationer who sits in hiding, enthroned behind her silver crates, an oriental veil of tinsel and cotton-wool Father Christmases drawn across her face. I discovered that the most beautiful of these stalls were on Arbatskaia Ploshchad [Square]. — A few days ago, a conversation in my room with Reich about journalism. Kisch[43] revealed some of its golden rules to him, to which I add a few of my own. 1) An article should contain as many names as possible. 2) The first and last sentences have to be good; the middle doesn't matter. 3) Use the fantasies that a name generates as the background for a description that represents it as it really is. I would like to collaborate with Reich here on drawing up a program for a materialist encyclopedia, about which he has some superb ideas. — Asja came by after seven.

43.   Egon Erwin Kisch (1885–1938) traveled in the Soviet Union from fall 1925 to spring 1926. He recorded his experiences in *Zaren, Popen, Bolschewiken*, Berlin, E. Reiss, 1927.

(But Reich came along to the theater.) They were performing Stanislavsky's production of *The Days of the Turbins*. The naturalistic style of the sets was remarkably good, the acting without any particular flaws or merits, Bulgakov's play itself an absolutely revolting provocation. Especially the last act, in which the white guards "convert" to bolshevism, is as dramatically insipid as it is intellectually mendacious. The communist opposition to the production is justified and significant. Whether this final act was added on at the request of the censors, as Reich claims, or whether it was there all along has no bearing whatsoever on the assessment of the play. (The audience was noticeably different from the ones I had seen in the other two theaters. It was as if there were not a single communist present, not a black or blue tunic in sight.) Our seats were not adjacent so I only sat next to Asja during the first tableau. Then Reich came to sit by me; he thought the strain of translating was too much for her.

December 15. Reich stepped out briefly after he got up and I hoped I would be able to greet Asja in private. But she never turned up. Reich learned in the afternoon that she had not been well that morning. But he wouldn't let me go see her in the afternoon either. We spent part of the morning together: he translated Kamenev's speech to the Comintern for me. — One only knows a spot once one has experienced it in as many dimensions as possible. You have to have approached a place from all four cardinal points if you want to take it in, and what's more, you also have to have left it from all these points. Otherwise it will quite unexpectedly cross your path three or four times before you are prepared to discover it. One stage further, and you seek it out, you orient yourself by it. The same thing with houses. It is only after having crept along a series of them in search of a very specific one that you come to learn what they contain. From the arches of gates, on the frames of house doors, in letters of varying sizes, black, blue, yellow, red, in the shape of arrows or in the image of boots or freshly-ironed laundry or a worn stoop or a stairway's solid landing, the life leaps out at you, combative, determined, mute. You have to have traveled the streets by streetcar to realize how this running battle continues up along the various stories and finally reaches its decisive pitch on the roofs. Only the strongest, most venerable slogans or commercial signboards manage to survive at this height and it is only from the air that one can survey the industrial elite of the town (here a few names) beneath one's eyes. — In the morning, visit St. Basil's Cathedral. The warm, cosy colors of its facade shine onto the snow. The regularity of its ground plan generated a construction whose symmetry cannot be visually grasped from any direction. This building is always holding something back, and could only be ambushed by the eye from the height of an airplane, against which its builders forgot to protect themselves. The inside of the church has not only been emptied, but eviscerated like a felled deer, and turned into a "museum" attraction for mass edification. With the removal of

t. Basil's Cathedral.

the interior furnishings — which, to judge by the surviving baroque altars, were for the most part artistically worthless — the brightly colored floral garlands that festoon all the corridors and vaults are hopelessly exposed; sadly enough, the no doubt more ancient painted stone of the inner chambers, which sparingly preserved the memory of the colorful spirals of the domes, has been distorted into rococo frivolity. The vaulted aisles are narrow, suddenly broadening into altar niches or circular chapels into which so little light pours from the elevated windows that one can barely make out the various devotional objects that have been allowed to remain. There is, however, a brightly lit little room, traversed by a red carpet, containing a display of icons by the schools of Moscow and Novgorod, as well as a few apparently priceless Gospels, and tapestries showing Adam and Christ in white against a green ground, naked, but bereft of genitals. The guard in this room is a fat woman with peasant looks. I would have liked to have heard the explanations of these pictures that she was offering to a number of proletarians. — Earlier, a short stroll through the arcades they call the "upper commercial lanes." I tried without success to buy some very interesting figurines — brightly colored clay horsemen — in the shopwindow of a toy store. Went to lunch by streetcar along the Moskova, passing the cathedral of the Redeemer, and across Arbatskaia Square. Returned there in the dark of the afternoon, walked around the rows of wooden booths, then down Frunze Street to the impressively elegant Ministry of War, ended up getting lost. Back home by streetcar. (Reich wanted to visit Asja on his own.) In the evening, across a sheet of fresh ice to Pansky's. Just as we reach his doorstep, he is in the process of leaving for the theater with his wife. On account of a misunderstanding which is only cleared up the following day, he asks us to come see him in his office within the next few days. Then to the big house on Strasnoi Square to visit an acquaintance of Reich's. In the elevator we meet the man's wife, who tells us he is at a meeting. But since Sofia's[44] mother lives in this same building — a sort of huge boarding house — we decide to drop in and say hello. Like all the rooms that I had seen so far (the ones at Granovsky's and Illés's), it contains only a few pieces of furniture. Their bleak, petit-bourgeois appearance is all the more depressing because the room is so sparsely furnished. Completeness is an essential feature of the decor of the petit-bourgeois interior: the walls must be covered with pictures, the sofa with cushions, the cushions with coverlets, the consoles with knickknacks, the windows with stained glass. Of all this only a few items here and there have indiscriminately survived. If people manage to bear rooms which look like infirmaries after inspection, it is because their way of life has so alienated them from domestic existence. The place in which they live is the office, the club, the street. To step into this room is immediately to realize that the astonish-

---

44.   Sofia Krylenko, sister of Nikolai Krylenko (1885–1938), Commissioner of Justice at that time. She was in Capri in 1924 at the same time as Benjamin and Lacis.

ing narrowness of Sofia's stubborn character is something she has inherited from her family, from whom she is estranged though not entirely severed. On the way back Reich tells me their story. Sofia's brother is Krylenko, the general who fought on the side of the Bolsheviks back in the beginning, rendering incalculable services to the Revolution. Since his political talents were quite limited, [they] later gave him an honorific position as public prosecutor. (He was also the prosecutor in the Kindermann case.)[45] Her mother is apparently also in some organization. She must be around seventy and still shows signs of considerable energy. It's under her that Sofia's children now have to suffer, shuttled back and forth between their grandmother and their aunt and not having seen their mother for years. Both children are the offspring of her first marriage to a nobleman who fought on the Bolshevik side during the civil war and died. The younger daughter was there when we arrived. She is extraordinarily pretty, very confident and graceful in her movements. She seems to be quite withdrawn. A letter from her mother had just arrived, and there was an argument with her grandmother because she had opened it even though it was not addressed to her. Sofia writes that she will not be permitted to remain in Germany any longer. Her family seems to have gotten wind of her illegal job; she is a calamity and her mother is visibly upset. A beautiful view from the room of the long string of lights down Tverskoi Boulevard.

December 16. I was writing my diary and had given up hope that Asja would stop by. Then she knocked. As she entered the room, I wanted to kiss her. As usual, it proved unsuccessful. I got out the card I had started to write to Bloch and handed it to her to add a note.[46] Another failed attempt to give her a kiss. I read what she had written. Questioned by her, I said: "Nicer than what you write me." And for this "impertinence," she kissed me, even hugging me in the process. We took a sleigh into town and visited a number of stores on Petrovka in order to buy fabric for her dress, her uniform. At least this is what I call it, since she insists that her new dress be exactly of the same cut as the old one from Paris. Initially went to a state store, the upper portions of whose walls featured scenes with cardboard figures encouraging the peasants and the workers to unite. The displays done in the saccharine taste so prevalent here: hammer and sickle, a cogwheel, and various other tools are, absurdly, executed in velvet-covered cardboard. This store contained only merchandise for peasants and proletarians. Of late, under the new "economic regime," these are

45.   Karl Kindermann was the primary defendant in a show trial of three young Germans who had been accused in October 1924 of conspiring to assassinate Lenin. Kindermann was condemned to death but the sentence was not carried out.
46.   The postcard never reached Ernst Bloch. It was returned as undeliverable, according to the letter to Siegfried Kracauer of February 23, 1927, reproduced in the appendix.

the only items the state factories produce.[47] The counters are mobbed. Other stores that are empty sell fabric only if paid for in coupons or — in cash — at prices beyond anybody's means. From a street vendor Asja helps me buy a small doll, a *vanka-vstanka*,[48] for Daga, although I primarily want to take advantage of the opportunity to get one for myself as well. From another vendor, a glass dove for the Christmas tree. We didn't, as far as I can tell, say much to each other. — Later with Reich in Pansky's office. He had led us to believe that he wanted to see us on an official matter. Since I was already there anyway, he pointed me in the direction of the screening room where two American journalists were being shown films. Unfortunately, having finally managed to gain admission after countless preliminaries, I arrived just as the screening of *Potemkin*[49] was coming to an end; all I saw was the final act. It was followed by *By the Law* — a film based on a story by London.[50] Its Moscow premiere, which had taken place a few days ago, had been a flop. Technically the film is good — its director, Kuleshov, has an excellent reputation. But the plot moves through such a succession of atrocities that its theme ends in absurdity. It is claimed that the anarchistic tendency of this film is directed against the right in general. Toward the end of the showing, Pansky himself came up to the screening room and then ushered me back into his office. The conversation would have gone on for some time had I not been afraid of missing Asja. It was too late for lunch anyway. When I got to the sanatorium, Asja had already left. I went home and shortly thereafter Reich arrived, soon followed by Asja. They had bought some presents for Daga, *valenki*, etc. In my room we got to talking about the "piano" as a piece of furniture that functions in the petit-bourgeois interior as the true dynamic center of all the dominant miseries and catastrophes of the household. Asja was electrified by the idea; she wanted to write an article on it with me which Reich would then turn into a dramatic sketch. For a few minutes Asja and I were alone. All I remember is that I said the words "preferably forever" and that she laughed so hard at this that I realized she had understood. In the evening, Reich took me to a vegetarian restaurant whose walls were covered with propaganda slogans. "No God — Religion is an Invention — No Creation," etc. Reich was unable to translate many of the references to *Das Kapital*. Later, back home, I managed to reach Roth [51] by tele-

47.   Not an allusion to Lenin's NEP (New Economic Policy), instituted in 1921, but to the *rezhim ekonomii* (austerity regime), a campaign to rationalize and reduce primary costs in all economic areas during the second half of the 1920s.
48.   A tumbler doll.
49.   *Bronenosets Potemkin* (*Battleship Potemkin*), 1925 film by Sergei Eisenstein (1898–1948).
50.   *Pozakonu* (*By the Law*), 1926 film by Lev Kuleshov (1899–1948), based on a story by Jack London. Kuleshov, a pioneer theorist and practitioner of montage, produced in this film, now considered a classic of the postrevolutionary cinema, a merciless condemnation of the institutions of bourgeois justice.
51.   Joseph Roth (1894–1939) had been commissioned by the *Frankfurter Zeitung* to report on his travels through the Soviet Union from late August through late December 1926. His report was

phone with Reich's assistance. He informed me that he was leaving town the following afternoon and, after some deliberation, I had no other choice but to accept his invitation to come dine at his hotel at eleven-thirty. Otherwise I could no longer have counted on speaking with him. Exhausted, I got into a sleigh around a quarter to twelve: Reich had spent the entire evening reading to me from his work. His essay on humanism, which admittedly is still in its early stages, is based on the very fruitful question: how was it that the French intelligentsia, which had prepared the battle of the great revolution, came to be disbanded so soon after 1792 and transformed into an instrument of the bourgeoisie? As we were discussing this, it occurred to me that the history of the "educated" ought to be materialistically presented as a function of and in close relation to a "history of uneducation." The origins of the latter are located in the modern period, at the moment when the medieval forms of domination cease to be at the same time the forms of education, whatever its (ecclesiastical) character, of the dominated. *Cuius regio eius religio* destroys the spiritual authority of the secular forms of domination. A history of this sort would show the process whereby, over the course of centuries, revolutionary energy is released from its religious cocoon by the uneducated classes, and the intelligentsia would be revealed to be not merely an army of deserters from the bourgeoisie but rather an advance guard of "uneducation." The sleigh ride refreshed me considerably. Roth was already sitting in the spacious dining room. With its blaring band, its two great palms only half the height of its ceiling, its brightly colored bars and buffets, and the sober refinement of its table settings, the place receives its guest like a European luxury hotel that has been transplanted far to the east. For the first time in Russia I drank vodka, we ate caviar, cold meat, and stewed fruit. When I look back over the entire evening, Roth makes a worse impression on me than he did in Paris. Or rather — more likely — I was already aware of these things in Paris, though they were still hidden, whereas this time they struck me as clear as day. The conversation we had started at dinner turned more intense when we went up to his suite. He began by reading me a long article on the Russian educational system.[52] I looked around the room, the table was littered with the leftovers of what appeared to have been a lavish tea which must have been served to at least three people. Roth apparently lives in grand style, the hotel suite — which is just as European in its appointments as is the restaurant — must cost a great deal, as did the fact-gathering tour that took him all the way to Siberia, the Caucasus, and Crimea. In the conversation that followed his reading, I pressed him to put his cards on the table. The long and the short of it: he had come to Russia as a (nearly) confirmed Bolshevik and was leaving it a royalist. As usual, the country is left

serialized as "Reise in Russland" in eighteen segments from September 1926 to January 1927.
52.   Roth's article "Die Schule und die Jugend" appeared in the *Frankfurter Zeitung* on January 18, 1927.

footing the bill for the change in color that occurs in the convictions of those who arrive here as scintillating reddish-pink politicians (under the banner of "leftwing" opposition or idiotic optimism). His face is all creased with wrinkles and has the unpleasant look of a snoop. I was struck the same way when I again met him at the Kameneva Institute (he had delayed his departure). I accepted his offer of a sleigh and was driven back to my hotel around two. There are bits of nightlife on the streets, in front of the big hotel and in front of a cafe. People band together in these spots, huddled against the cold.

December 17. A visit to Daga. She looks better than I have ever seen her. The discipline of the children's home is having a powerful effect on her. Her gaze is quiet and assured, her face much fuller and less nervous. Her striking similarity to Asja has become less pronounced. The classrooms were most interesting, their walls thickly covered in places with drawings and cardboard figures. A kind of temple wall to which the children offer their own work as gifts to the collective. Red is the predominant color in these spots. They are interspersed with Soviet stars and heads of Lenin. In the classrooms the children do not sit at desks but instead at tables with long benches. They say *"Zdravstvuitie"* when you enter. Since the establishment does not provide them with clothing, many of them look quite poor. Near the sanatorium there are other children playing who come from nearby farms. Travel to Mytishchi[53] and back via sleigh, against the wind. Afternoon in the sanatorium with Asja, in a very foul mood. A six-way domino game in the recreation room. Evening meal with Reich in a pastry shop, a cup of coffee and cake. In bed early.

December 18. Asja came by in the morning. Reich had already left. We went to buy the fabric after having changed money at the Gosbank. While we were still in my room, I mentioned yesterday's mood to Asja. Things went well this morning, as well as was to be expected. The fabric was very expensive. On our return home, we happened on a crew shooting a film. Asja told me this should really be described, the way people immediately lose their heads on these occasions and tag along for hours and then get to their offices all flustered, unable to explain where they have been. You realize how true this is when you observe how many times a meeting has to be arranged here before it finally takes place. Nothing ever happens as planned or expected — this banal formulation of life's complications is borne out so implacably and so intensely in every single instance here that you quickly come to grasp the fatalism of the Russians. However slowly the calculable advance of civilization progresses within the collectivity, its initial effects will only further complicate individual existence. One

---

53.   A village on the Yauza River (Moscow district).

is better off in a house that only has candles than in one that has electric lights that don't work because of constant power failures. There are also people here who couldn't care what things are called and simply accept them as they are, children for example, lacing their skates on the street. Hazards of streetcar travel here. Through the iced-over windows you can never make out where you are. If you do find out, then the way to the exit is blocked by a mass of bulkily clad people. Since you get on at the rear but leave from the head of the car, you have to work your way through the crowd and your success depends on sheer luck and on the uninhibited use of physical force. On the other hand, there are conveniences here unknown to Western Europe. The state grocery stores remain open until eleven at night and the apartment buildings until midnight or later. There are too many tenants and subtenants: they can't all be provided with their own keys. — It has been observed that pedestrians here walk in "zigzags." This is simply on account of the overcrowding of the narrow sidewalks; nowhere else, except here and there in Naples, do you find sidewalks this narrow. They give Moscow a provincial air, or rather the character of an improvised metropolis that has fallen into place overnight. — We bought some good brown fabric. Then I went to the Institute, procured a voucher for the Meyerhold and also met Roth. After lunch I played chess with Reich in Dom Herzena. Then Kogan arrived with the reporter. I made up something about wanting to do a book dealing with art under dictatorships: Italian art under the Fascist regime and Russian art under the dictatorship of the proletariat. I went on to speak about Scheerbart's and Emil Ludwig's books.[54] Reich was extremely upset with the interview and explained that I had, through my needless theoretical expostulations, dangerously laid myself open to attack. So far the interview has not yet appeared (I'm writing this on the 21st), one will have to wait for the reactions. — Asja was not feeling well. A patient who had lost her mind after an attack of cerebrospinal meningitis and whom she previously knew from the hospital had been placed in the room next to hers. In the course of the night, Asja stirred up a rebellion among the other women, with the result that the patient was removed. Reich took me to the Meyerhold Theater where I met Fanny Elovaya.[55] But the Institute is on poor terms with Meyerhold: it had not called ahead of time and we were unable to get tickets. After a brief stop in my hotel, we drove to the vicinity of the Krasnaia Vorota [Red Gate] to see a film which Pansky had claimed would outdo the success of *Potemkin*. It was sold out. We got tickets for the next showing and went to Elovaya's nearby apartment to have some tea. The room was just as bare as all the ones I had seen so far. On its gray wall, the large photograph showing

54.   Emil Ludwig (1881–1948), prolific German biographer and historian. Paul Scheerbart (1863–1915), German essayist and novelist, author of Utopian novels and science fiction; Benjamin and Scholem particularly admired his book *Glasarchitektur* (1914).
55.   Probably Nina Yermolaeva; she played the role of Avdotiza in Meyerhold's production of *The Inspector General*.

Lenin reading *Pravda*. A few books on a narrow stand, two wicker suitcases against the dividing wall near the door, and along the two outer walls, a bed faced by a table and two chairs. The time spent in this room with a cup of tea and a piece of bread was the best part of the evening. The film turned out to be an unbearable botch and they projected it at such a dizzying speed that it was impossible to watch or understand. We left before it was over. The return home by streetcar was like some episode out of the inflation era. I found Reich in my room, he again spent the night there.

December 19. I can't exactly remember the events of the morning. I think I saw Asja and then wanted to go to the Tretiakov gallery after having taken her back to the sanatorium. But I could not find her and wandered in the bitter cold through the construction sites, parade grounds, and churches on the left bank of the Moskva. I watched the Red Army soldiers drilling as children played soccer between their ranks. Young girls emerged from a school. Across from the stop where I finally took a streetcar home, there was a luminous red church with a long red wall extending to the street, a tower and domes. I was all the more drained by my wanderings because I was carrying an unwieldy package containing three little houses made out of colored paper, which, for the enormous price of thirty kopeks, I had with great difficulty procured from a stall on one of the main streets of the left bank. Afternoon at Asja's. I went out to get her some cakes. As I was standing in the door about to leave, I was struck by Reich's odd behavior, he did not respond to my "good-bye." I assumed he was in a bad mood. When he had earlier left the room for a few minutes, I had assured Asja that he would certainly be getting the cakes, and when he came back she had been disappointed. When I returned with the cakes a few minutes later, Reich was lying on the bed. He had had a heart attack. Asja was very agitated. It struck me that Asja was dealing with Reich's ailment the same way I used to deal with Dora when she was sick. She was scolding him, trying to help out in a thoughtless, provocative manner, acting like someone who wants to make the other person aware just how guilty he is for having gotten sick. Reich slowly recovered. But this unfortunate incident meant that I had to go to the Meyerhold Theater alone. Later Asja brought Reich back to my room. He spent the night in my bed and I slept on the sofa that Asja had made up for me. — Even though it had been shortened by an hour following its premier, *The Inspector General* still ran from quarter to eight until midnight. The play was divided into three parts, with a total of (if I'm not mistaken) sixteen tableaux.[56] Reich's many accounts had prepared me for the overall visual effect of the production. Nonetheless I was amazed at its extravagance. In fact, the most remarkable thing about the production was not its sumptuous costuming but

56.   In fact there were fifteen episodes.

Final tableau from Meyerhold's The Inspector General.
(Photo courtesy Harvard Theater Collection.)

rather the stage sets.[57] With very few exceptions, the scenes were played on a tiny area of an inclined plane on which, at every shift of scene, the sets would change into different Empire-style mahogany decors with different furnishings. The net effect of this was the creation of a number of charming genre pictures, which is in accordance with the basic intent of this nondramatic, sociologically analytical production. People ascribe a great deal of importance to this production as an adaptation of a classical play for the revolutionary theater, but they also consider the experiment a failure. The Party, moreover, has come out against the production, and even the moderate review by *Pravda*'s theater critic was rejected by the editors. The applause in the theater was restrained, and perhaps this was due to the official line more than to the audience's actual reaction. Certainly the production was a feast for the eyes. But this is no doubt linked to the general atmosphere of cautiousness here when it comes to openly revealing one's opinions. If you ask people whom you barely know what they think of some insignificant play or film, the answer is: "the word here is this or that," or "people have mostly been of such and such an opinion." The guiding principle of this production, the concentration of the action into an extremely restricted area, creates an extraordinarily luxurious density of dramatic values,

57.   The stage design was by Meyerhold together with Viktor Kiselev (1895–?), who designed the costumes and assembled the stage objects, most prominently the antiques. Kiselev had also collaborated on Meyerhold's second production of *Mystery-Bouffe*.

without, however, neglecting the acting dimension. The high point of all this came in a party scene, which was a masterpiece of staging. There were about fifteen people huddled on the tiny performance area, grouped between barely suggested pillars made of paper. (Reich spoke of the abolition of linear arrangement.) On the whole, the effect is like the architecture of a cake (a very Muscovite simile — only the cakes here could explain the comparison), or better yet, like the grouping of dancing puppets on a musical clock whose strains are played by Gogol's text. There is, moreover, a great deal of actual music in the play, and the little quadrille that occurs toward the end would be an attractive number in any bourgeois theater; in a proletarian one it comes somewhat as a surprise. The latter's forms are most clearly evident in a scene in which a long balustrade divides the stage in two; the Inspector General stands in front of it, while the masses remain behind, watching his every movement and playing a very expressive game with his coat — now grabbing it with six or eight hands, now tossing it over the shoulders of the Inspector General as he leans against the parapet. — Slept quite well on the hard bed.

December 20. I'm writing on the 23rd and no longer remember the events of the morning. Instead of sketching them, a few notes on Asja and our relationship, even though Reich is sitting right next to me. I find myself facing an almost impregnable fortress. Nonetheless I tell myself that my mere appearance before this fortress, Moscow, already constitutes an initial triumph. But any further, decisive victory seems almost insurmountably difficult. Reich's position is strong, given the obvious successes which he has managed to register in quick succession after an extremely difficult period of six months, during which, not knowing the language, he was freezing and perhaps even going hungry. This morning he told me that after half a year he had hopes for a position here. He is less enthusiastic about Moscow's working conditions than is Asja, but he manages more easily. During the initial period after her arrival from Riga, Asja even considered moving back to Europe immediately, so hopeless did the job situation seem to her. When she finally landed work at the children's school, it was only a matter of a few weeks before she was put out of commission by her illness. Had she not obtained her union membership one or two days earlier, she would have received no medical care and might possibly have died. It is obvious that, even now, she is still attracted to Western Europe. It is not merely the attraction of travel, foreign cities, the amenities of cosmopolitan bohemianism, but also the liberating influence her thinking underwent in Western Europe, especially through her contacts with Reich and me. Indeed, as Reich was lately saying, it's fairly mysterious how, being here in Russia, Asja managed to develop the acuity of insight which she was already displaying in Western Europe. For me, Moscow is now a fortress; the harsh climate which is wearing me down, no matter how healthy it might be for me, my ignorance of the language, Reich's presence, Asja's utterly circumscribed mode of existence all constitute so many bastions, and it is only the total impossibility of advancing any further, only the fact that Asja's illness, or at least her weakness, pushes our personal affairs into the background, that keeps me from becoming completely depressed by all this. Whether I will achieve the secondary purpose of my journey — to escape the deadly melancholy of the Christmas season — remains to be seen. If I am still holding out fairly well, it is also because despite everything, I recognize Asja's attachment to me. The familiar *Du* seems to have gained ground between us, and the long gazes she directs at me — I cannot remember a woman granting gazes or kisses this long — have lost none of their power over me. Today I told her that I now wanted to have a child by her. Certain gestures, spontaneous yet rare and not without significance given the control she has now imposed on herself in erotic matters, tell me she is fond of me. Just yesterday, as I was in the process of leaving her room to avoid an argument, she grabbed hold of me violently and ran her hands through my hair. Also, she often says my name. At one point in the past few days she said it was entirely my fault that we were not now living on a "desert isle" and didn't have two children. There is some truth to this. On three or four occasions, I directly or indirectly avoided sharing a future with her: when I didn't "run off" with her in Capri, but how? — when I refused to accompany her from Rome to Assisi and Orvieto, when I didn't follow her to Latvia in the summer of 1925 and didn't want to be tied down waiting for her in Berlin that winter. What came into play were not the financial considerations, nor even the fanatic urge to travel, which has since diminished in me over the past two years, but rather the fear of those hostile elements in her which only now do I feel I can confront. In the past few days I also said to her that had we decided to join together back then, I don't know that we wouldn't have split up long ago. Everything happening in and around me combines to make the idea of living apart from her more intolerable to me than it ever was before. A contributing factor is certainly the fear that in the future, when Asja is finally well again and living here with Reich on stable terms, it will only be with a considerable amount of pain that I will be able to come up against the boundaries of our relationship. I still don't know if I will be able to disengage myself from it. At this point, I have no cause to sever myself from her completely, even admitting I were capable of it. The thing I would prefer the most would be the bond a child might create between us. But I have no idea whether I could even now bear living with her, given her astonishing hardness and, despite all her sweetness, her lovelessness. — Life here in the winter is richer by a dimension: space literally changes according to whether it is hot or cold. People live on the street as if in a frosty hall of mirrors, and every decision, every stop becomes incredibly difficult: it takes half a day of deliberation to go drop a letter in a mailbox, and despite the bitter cold, it takes an effort of the will to enter a store to buy something. Apart from a gigantic foodstore on Tverskaia which features luminous displays of prepared dishes such as I have only seen in the illustrations of my mother's cookbooks and whose sumptuousness outstrips anything comparable from the czarist era, the shops do not invite lingering. Plus they are provincial. You rarely encounter signs emblazoned with the name of the firm visible from afar, as is the case on the main streets of Western cities; for the most part, they merely indicate the kind of merchandise for sale, with an occasional watch, suitcase, boot, fur, etc. painted on the signs. The traditional stretched hide of the tanner is daubed on a tin shield. Shirts are usually painted on a board bearing the words *Kitaiskaia Prachechnaia* — Chinese laundry. One sees many beggars. They direct lengthy supplications at passers-by. One of them breaks into a low howl each time he senses the potential largess of a passing pedestrian. I also saw a beggar in exactly the same pose as the miserable creature for whom St. Martin cut his cloak in two with a sword, on his knees, his arm outstretched. Shortly before Christmas, there were two children on Tverskaia always sitting in the same spot against the wall of the Museum of the Revolution, covered in rags, whimpering. This would seem to be an expression of the infinite misery of these beggars, but it may also be the result of clever organization, for of all the Moscow institutions they alone are reliable, they alone refuse to be budged. Everything else here takes place under the banner of the *remont*.[58] Every week the furniture in the bare rooms gets rearranged — this is the sole domestic luxury in which one can indulge and at the same time it provides a radical means of ridding the home of "coziness" and the attendant melancholia that is its price. Government offices, museums, and institutes are forever changing location, and even the street vendors, who in other cities have their fixed spots, turn up in different places every day. Everything, shoe polish, picture books, stationery, pastries and breads, even towels, is sold out in the open on the street, as if the minus twenty-five degree Moscow winter were in fact a Neapolitan summer. — Visiting Asja in the afternoon, I mentioned that I wanted to write on theater for the *Literarische Welt*. There was a short argument, but then I invited her to play dominos with me. Finally she consented: "If you should so request. I am weak. I cannot refuse anybody's request." But later, when Reich arrived, Asja again led the conversation back to the same subject and a tremendous quarrel broke out. It was only upon leaving, as I was standing up from my window niche and getting ready to catch up with Reich on the street, that Asja took my hand and said: "It's not all that bad." Another short argument about the matter in my room that evening. Then he went home.

December 21. I walked the entire length of the Arbat and reached the market on Smolensk Boulevard. The day was extremely cold. As I walked I ate some

---

58.   Russian, deriving from French, for "repair"; an allusion to the profusion of small shops for the repair of household articles and implicitly to the paucity of consumer goods.

chocolate that I had bought along the way. The first row of the market which is set up along the street was comprised of booths selling Christmas items, toys, and paper articles. The row behind this was devoted to iron wares, household goods, shoes, etc. It somewhat resembled the market on Arbatskaia Ploschad, but I don't believe they sold any food provisions here. But even before you reach the booths, the path is so crowded with baskets of delicacies, tree decorations, and toys that you can barely make your way from the street to the sidewalk. I bought a kitsch postcard in one of the booths, and a balalaika and little paper house in one of the others. Here as well I observed Christmas roses on the street, heroic bunches of flowers brightly shining forth from the ice and snow. I had a difficult time finding my way to the toy museum with all my

Smolensk bazaar.

purchases. It had been moved from Smolensk Boulevard to ulitsa Krapot-
kina, and when I had finally managed to locate it, I was so exhausted that I
almost turned back at the entrance: the door did not give immediately and I
was convinced it was locked. Afternoon at Asja's. Went to a terrible play in the
evening at the Korsh Theater (*Alexander I and Ivan Kuzmich*).[59] Its author but-
tonholed Reich during one of the breaks — he described the hero of his play as
a spiritual cousin of Hamlet — and it was only with difficulty that, escaping his
vigilance, we managed to avoid the final acts. After the theater, if I remember
well, we had something additional to eat. Reich slept at my place.

December 22. In the course of discussions with Reich, I hit upon a number of important things. In the evenings we often talk at great length about Russia,
theater, materialism. Reich is very disappointed with Plekhanov. I tried to explain to him the opposition between materialist and universalist modes of
representation. The universalist mode is always idealistic because undialecti-
cal. Dialectic in fact inevitably moves toward representing each thesis or anti-
thesis that it encounters as the fresh synthesis of a triadic structure, and in this
way it penetrates ever deeper into the interior of the object and only via the latter does it represent a universe. Any other concept of a universe is without object, idealist. I furthermore attempted to ascribe Plekhanov's nonmaterialist
thinking to the role played by theory in his work, and I referred to the opposition between theory and method. In its effort to represent what is general,
theory hovers above science, whereas it is characteristic of method that every
examination of a universal principle immediately discovers its own specific object. (Example: the examination of the concepts of time and space in relativity
theory.) On another occasion, a discussion about the notion of success as the
decisive criterion for "average" authors, and about the specific structure of
"greatness" among great writers — who are "great" because their effect is
historical, but who, conversely, had no effect on history through their literary
powers. How one only sees these "great" authors magnified and tinted by the
lenses of one's own century. And furthermore: how this contributes to an absolutely conservative attitude toward authorities and yet how precisely this conservative attitude can be established solely from a materialist perspective. On
another occasion, we spoke together of Proust (I read to him from my translation),[60] and then of Russian cultural policies: the "education program" for

---

59.   Theater founded by Fyodor Korsh (1852–1923); it was incorporated into the state theater
system in 1925–1926, and closed in 1932.
60.   Benjamin was working on a translation of *Le cote de Guermantes*, the third volume of Proust's
A la recherche du temps perdu. It was published in 1930, with Franz Hessel as cotranslator, by Piper
Verlag in Munich. Benjamin and Hessel had previously collaborated on a translation of volume
two, *A l'ombre des jeunes filles en fleurs*, published in 1927 by Verlag Die Schmiede in Berlin. In addition,
Benjamin apparently translated volume four, *Sodome et Gomorrhe*, on his his own, but this trans-

workers devised to render all of world literature accessible to them, the exclusion of leftwing writers who had been at the helm back in the days of heroic communism, the encouragement of reactionary peasant art (the AKHRR exhibition).[61] All of this again struck me as very relevant when I was visiting the office of the *Encyclopedia* that afternoon with Reich. This undertaking is projected to include some thirty or forty volumes, with a special volume dedicated specifically to Lenin. When we got there (the second time, our first visit had been in vain), there was a very well-meaning young man sitting behind a desk to whom Reich — praising my qualifications — introduced me. As I outlined the scheme of my "Goethe" to him, his intellectual insecurity immediately became evident. There were a number of things in my proposal that intimidated him, and he finally ended up recommending a biographical portrait against a sociological background. But it is fundamentally impossible to do a materialist depiction of a writer's life, one can only show its historical aftereffects. In fact, if abstracted from its posterity, an artist's existence and even his purely temporal oeuvre can offer no object whatsoever for materialist analysis. It is probably this same unmethodological universality and immediacy that characterizes the totally idealistic, metaphysical questions addressed by Bukharin's *Introduction to Historical Materialism*.[62] With Asja in the afternoon. A Jewish communist has recently moved into her room and they get on very well and do a great deal of talking together. I find Asja's presence less agreeable because now, even when Reich is not around, I rarely speak to her in private anymore. Evening at home.

December 23. I was at the Kustarny Museum[63] in the morning. There were again very beautiful toys to be seen; the director of the toy museum has also organized the exhibit here. The papier-mâché figures are perhaps the most beautiful. They are often supported by a small pedestal or by a tiny hurdy-gurdy with a handle that turns or by an inclined plane that can be compressed and emits a sound. There are also very large figures of the same material that represent types easily verging on the grotesque and that already belong to a period of decadence. In the museum there was a shabbily dressed, attractive girl discussing the toys in French with two small boys whose governess she was. All three

lation has been lost. Benjamin and Hessel planned to translate the entire work (they began the translation of the fifth volume, *La Prisonnière*), but the project was never realized. See R. Piper, *Briefwechsel mit Autoren und Künstlern 1903–1953*, Munich, Piper, 1979, pp. 213–220.

61.   Assotsiatsiia Khudozhnikov Revolutsionnoi Rossii (Association of Russian Revolutionary Artists), 1922–1932. The AKHRR campaigned against formalism and promoted realist-naturalist genre painting.
62.   Nikolai Bukharin (1888–1938), member of the executive committee of the Comintern, 1926–1930, and editor-in-chief of *Izvestia*. His *Theory of Historical Materialism* appeared in 1922.
63.   Museum of Arts and Crafts.

were Russian. The museum has two halls. The larger one, which also contains the toys, features in addition examples of lacquerwork and textiles, the smaller one contains ancient wood sculptures, boxes in the shape of ducks or other animals, tools, etc., and wrought-iron work. In the downstairs storage area that is contiguous to the museum, I was unable to discover any object whatsoever that was representative of ancient toys. On the other hand, I saw a store of tree decorations such as I had never encountered before. Then I went to the Kameneva Institute to pick up tickets for *Les*[64] and I met Basseches.[65] We walked together for a stretch and it was three-thirty when I finally got to Dom Herzena. Reich arrived even later, after I had already finished my meal. I ordered a second cup of coffee, vowing to myself that I wouldn't touch it. In the afternoon there was a game of dominos, and for the first time I was teamed up with Asja. We brilliantly defeated Reich and her roommate. The latter I met up with later at the Meyerhold Theater, while Reich was attending a meeting of VAPP. She spoke Yiddish to make herself understood. The thing might have been feasible with a little more practice, but as it was, I couldn't get much out of it. The evening was very tiring; either owing to some slip-up or to her lack of punctuality, we arrived late and had to stand through the first act in the back row. Then there was also the Russian. Asja didn't get to sleep until her roommate returned. But then, so she told me the next day, the latter's regular breathing had put her to sleep. The celebrated harmonica scene in *Les*[66] is truly quite beautiful, but it had become so spendidly and romantically lodged in my imagination through Asja's description of it that I initially had difficulty finding my way into it when I encountered its reality on stage. The whole production is full of splendid moments: the scene in which the eccentric ham actor is fishing and creates the illusion of the catch wriggling on his line with the mere quivers of his hand, the love scene that is played out as they run in a circle, the entire scene on the catwalk that leads down to the stage from a scaffold. For the first time I clearly grasped the function of the constructivist use of the stage; it had never been this evident to me at Tairov's in Berlin[67] and even less so in photographs.

---

64. *The Forest*, by Alexandr Ostrovsky (1832–1886). The premiere of Meyerhold's production of the play took place on January 19, 1924.
65. Nikolaus Basseches (1895–1961), Austrian journalist and engineer. Born in Moscow, the son of the Austrian consul general, he wrote for Austrian newspapers and worked with the Austrian legation in Moscow. During the 1940s he lived in Switzerland and wrote on Soviet affairs for the *Weltwoche* and the *Neue Zürcher Zeitung*. His books include *Das wirtschaftliche Gesicht der Soviet-Union*, Vienna, C. Gerolds Sohn, 1925; in English translation, *The Unknown Army: The Nature and History of the Russian Military Forces*, New York, Viking, 1943; and *Stalin*, New York, Dutton, 1952.
66. There is no "harmonica scene" in the original version of *Les*. A scene of this sort occurs only in Meyerhold's adaptation and corresponds to the original act 4, scene 5.
67. Alexandr Tairov's theater troupe played Berlin in 1923.

December 24. A few words about my room. Every piece of furniture in it bears a tin tag with the words *Moscow Hotels* and then the inventory number. The hotels are collectively administered by the state (or the city?). The double windows of my room have been sealed shut for the winter. Only a small flap toward the top can be opened. The small washtable is made of tin, lacquered below and with a very polished top and a mirror in addition. The bottom of the basin has three drain holes that cannot be plugged. A thin stream of water flows from a faucet. The room is heated from the exterior, but given its particular location, the floor is also warm and even when the weather is moderately cold, the heat becomes oppressive as soon as you close the little window. Every morning before nine, when the heat is turned on, an employee knocks at the door to check if the trap window has been shut. This is the only thing that one can rely on here. The hotel has no kitchen, so one can't even get a cup of tea. Once, the evening before we drove out to see Daga, we asked to be awakened the following morning, and a Shakespearian conversation on the theme of "waking" ensued between Reich and the Swiss (which is the Russian name for hotel porter). The man's reply to our request to be awakened: "If we think of it, we'll wake you. But if we don't think of it, we won't. Actually, we usually think of it, in which case we do wake people. But to be sure, we also occasionally forget to when we don't think of it. In which case we don't. We're of course under no obligation, but if we remember in time, then naturally we do. When do you want to be awakened? — At seven. We'll make a note of that. See, I'm putting the message here, let's hope he finds it. Of course if he doesn't, he won't wake you. But usually we in fact do." In the end we were of course not wakened and they explained: "You were already up, what was the point of waking you?" There seems to be no shortage of these Swiss in the hotel. They all sit around in a little room on the ground floor. The other day Reich asked one of them if there was any mail for me. The man said no, even though the letters were lying there in front of his nose. On another occasion someone tried to reach me at the hotel by telephone, only to be told: "He has since checked out." The telephone is in the corridor and from my bed I often hear long conversations going on at night even after one o'clock. The bed has a big pit in its middle and the slightest movement is enough to make it creak. Since Reich often snores so loudly at night that he wakes me up, it would be very difficult to sleep were it not for the fact that I always go to bed dead tired. When I'm here afternoons I fall asleep. The hotel bill has to be paid daily because there is a ten percent tax on any account over five rubles. The incredible waste of time and energy this involves is self-evident. — Reich and Asja had met on the street and arrived together. Asja was not feeling well and had canceled the evening with Birse. They wanted to spend it with me. She had brought along her fabric; and then we went out. I took her to her dressmaker before going on to the toy museum. On our way we stopped at a watchmaker's. Asja gave him my watch. He was a Jew who spoke German. After taking leave of Asja, I went to the

museum by sleigh. I was afraid I would arrive late, not yet having adjusted to
the Russian sense of time. A tour of the toy museum. My guide, *tov.* [*arishch*]
Bartram,[68] presented me with a copy of his study, *From Toy to Children's Theater*,
which would become my Christmas present to Asja. Then to the Academy,
but Kogan was not there. I was going to return by bus and had posted myself at
my stop. Then I saw the word *Museum* inscribed over an open door and soon
realized that I was facing the "second collection of modern Western art." I had
not intended to visit this museum. But since I was standing in front of it, I went
in. As I was looking at an extraordinarily beautiful Cézanne, it suddenly occurred to me that it is even linguistically fallacious to speak of "empathy." It
seemed to me that to the extent that one grasps a painting, one does not in any
way enter into its space; rather, this space thrusts itself forward, especially in
various very specific spots. It opens up to us in corners and angles in which we
believe we can localize crucial experiences of the past; there is something in-
explicably familiar about these spots. This painting hung on the middle wall of
the first of the two Cézanne rooms, directly across from the window, full of
light. It depicts a road running through a wood. There is a group of houses to
one side. The museum's Renoir collection is not as outstanding as its Cézanne
holdings. Nonetheless it contains a number of his early paintings that are very
fine. But what moved me most in the first two rooms were two paintings of the
Paris boulevards, hanging, like pendants, across from each other. One is by
Pissarro, the other by Monet. Both of them render the broad street from an
elevated perspective, which in the first painting is situated in the center, while
in the second the point of view is more oblique. So oblique in fact that the
silhouettes of two gentlemen who are leaning out over the street from a balcony
railing seem to sidle into the picture as if they were right next to the window
where the scene is being painted. And whereas the gray asphalt with its innum-
erable horse and carriages extends over the major portion of the picture plane
in Pissarro's case, in the Monet half the plane is taken up by the luminous wall
of a house which half shimmers through yellow autumnal trees. At the foot of
this house can be discerned, half hidden by the leaves, the chairs and tables of a
cafe, sitting there like rustic furniture in a sunny forest. But Pissarro conveys
the space of Paris, the line of the roofs with their thick crop of chimneys. I felt
his nostalgia for this city. — In one of the rear rooms near drawings by Louis
Legrand and Degas, a painting by Odilon Redon. — After the bus ride back, I
wandered about at length and, one hour after the appointed time, I finally
made it to the cellar restaurant where Reich and I had agreed to meet. Since it
was already near four o'clock, we immediately had to go our separate ways and
agreed to rendezvous later in the big food emporium on Tverskaia. It was
only a few hours before Christmas Eve and the store was mobbed. As we were

68.   Nikolai D. Bartram (1873–1934?)

buying caviar, lox, and fruit, we ran into Basseches carrying packages. In high spirits. Reich's mood on the other hand was awful. He was quite irritated that I had arrived so late, and a Chinese paper fish that I had acquired on the street that morning and which I had been lugging around in addition to all my other things only served, by providing proof of my mania for collecting, to exasperate him further. We went on to procure cakes and sweets, as well as a small tree decorated with garlands, and I took the load home by sleigh. Darkness had long since fallen. I was worn out from fighting my way through the crowds with my tree and my packages. Back in my room, I lay down on the bed and read Proust while eating some of the candied nuts we had bought because they are a favorite of Asja's. Reich arrived after seven, Asja came somewhat later. She spent the whole evening lying on the bed and Reich sat next to her on a chair. After a long wait, a samovar finally arrived — our earlier requests for one had been futile because apparently a guest had locked all of them in his room and had then gone off — and hearing its hum fill a Russian room for the first time, able to look straight into Asja's face as she lay there across from me, sitting next to the little potted pine tree, I experienced something I had not felt in years, a sense of security on Christmas Eve. We spoke of the job that Asja was to have taken, then talk turned to my book on the *Trauerspiel*, and I read aloud from the preface directed against the University of Frankfurt.[69] Asja's opinion may take on importance for me; she thought that despite everything I should simply write: rejected by the University of Frankfurt-on-Main. We were very close that evening. Asja got a lot of laughs out of some of the things I was saying to her. Other things, such as the idea for an article on German philosophy as a tool of German domestic politics, excited her intense approbation. She couldn't make up her mind to leave, she was feeling good and tired. But in the end it was not even eleven when she left. I went right to bed because my evening had been full, however short it may have been. I realized that solitude does not exist for us as long as someone we love, even though they be somewhere else well beyond our reach, is feeling alone at the same time. The feeling of solitude would therefore seem to be basically a reflexive phenomenon that only strikes us when emitted back to us by people we know, and most often by people we love, whenever they enjoy themselves socially without us. And even the person who feels fundamentally alone in the world only experiences his solitude when he thinks of a woman, even an unknown woman, or of anybody else who is not alone and in whose company he, too, would cease to be.

69.   Benjamin wished to present his *Ursprung des deutschen Trauerspiels* (Berlin, Rowohlt, 1928; translated as *The Origin of German Tragic Drama*, London, New Left Books, 1977) as a habilitation thesis at the University of Frankfurt, but feeling it likely to be rejected, withdrew it. The preface he alludes to here is not the book's "Epistemo-Critical Preface," but a preliminary note—a bitter fairy tale about Benjamin's prickly relation to academia—that he eliminated from the published version.

December 25. I have resigned myself to getting by with the little bit of Russian that I manage to stutter out and have decided not to continue studying it because I badly need the time for other things: for translating and for articles. Should I ever return to Russia, it will obviously be essential that I bring some previously acquired knowledge of the language along with me. But since I have no plan of attack for the future at the moment, I'm not absolutely certain about all this: in other circumstances that might well be less favorable than the present ones, things could perhaps become all too difficult for me. At the very least, there would have to be very solid literary and financial arrangements before I undertook a second trip to Russia. My ignorance of Russian has never been as disturbing and tormenting to me as it was on the first day of the Christmas celebrations. We were having dinner with Asja's roommate — I had donated the money for a goose; this had caused an argument between Asja and me a few days earlier. Now plates with individual portions of goose were being brought to the table. It was badly cooked, tough. The meal was served on a writing desk around which six to eight people were sitting. Only Russian was being spoken. The cold appetizer, a fish prepared Jewish style, was good, as was the soup. After the meal, I went into the next room and dozed off. I continued lying on the sofa for a while, now awake and very sad, seized, as was so often the case, by images of the times I went up to Seeshaupt from Munich during my student days.[70] Afterwards, Reich or Asja occasionally tried to translate a snatch of the conversation for me, but this only made it doubly strenuous. For a while they were discussing the fact that the War Academy had given a professorship to a general who had once been a white guard and had ordered the hanging of every Red Army member captured in the civil war. They argued about what position should be taken on this. The most orthodox person there was a very fanatic young Bulgarian woman. It finally came time to leave, Reich leading the way with the Bulgarian woman, Asja and I following behind. I was totally exhausted. There was no streetcar service that day. And since Reich and I could not accompany them by bus, we had no choice but to go the long stretch to the second MKHAT on foot. Reich wanted to see the performance of the *Oresteia* there in order to gather further material for his piece on "The Counterrevolution on the Stage." They gave us seats in the center of the second row. A waft of perfume greeted me as I entered the theater. I did not see a single communist in a blue tunic, but there were several types who would not have been out of place in any of George Grosz's albums. The entire production was done in the style of a dusty court theater. The director not only lacked any professional expertise, but possessed not even the most elementary fund of information

70.   According to Gershom Scholem in *Walter Benjamin: The Story of a Friendship*, Philadelphia, Jewish Publication Society of America, 1981, Benjamin began visiting his future wife Dora (then still married to Max Pollak) at her villa at Seeshaupt on Lake Starnberg in early 1916.

necessary to the staging of Aeschylus. A bloodless, drawing-room Hellenism seems fully to satisfy his impoverished imagination. The music played on almost without interruption and included a great deal of Wagner: *Tristan*, the "Magic Fire Music."

December 26. Asja's stay in the sanatorium seems to be reaching its end. Over the past few days the hours she has spent lying outdoors have proved beneficial. She likes to lie there in her sack of blankets and listen to the crows in the air. She is even convinced that the birds have organized themselves with great precision and that their leader informs them as to what to do; certain birdcalls preceded by a long pause are, according to her, orders that they all follow. I have barely spoken to Asja in private of late, but in the few words we do exchange I believe I detect her closeness to me so distinctly that I feel a great sense of calm and well-being. I can think of nothing that has as healing and yet as intense an effect on me as the most trivial little questions she puts to me about my affairs. To be sure, she doesn't do this often. But on this day, for example, she turned to me in the middle of a meal where only Russian was being spoken and asked me what mail had arrived for me the previous day. Before eating, three of us had played dominos together. Things went far better after the meal than they had the previous day. They sang communist adaptations (I don't believe they were intended as parodies) of Yiddish songs. Except for Asja, everybody in the room was certainly Jewish. There was also a trade-union secretary there who had come to Moscow for the seventh Congress of Trade Unionists. It was early when we took Asja home. I invited Reich out for a cup of coffee before going home. And then he started in: the more he looked around, the more he realized what immense pests children were. There had been a young and moreover very well-behaved boy present at the comrade's place, and as we were all sitting around playing dominos, having already waited two hours to eat, he had begun to cry. But in reality the child that was on Reich's mind was Daga. He spoke of Asja's chronic bouts of anxiety, which for the most were focused on Daga, and he went into the whole story of her Moscow residence once again. I had often marveled at the patience he showed in dealing with her. And even now he was not showing the slightest traces of ill humor or bitterness, only the tension that this talk with me was releasing. He lamented the fact that Asja's "egoism" was failing her precisely now that everything depended on taking it easy and letting things follow their course. Her anxiety about where to live next, the thought that it would most probably entail moving, greatly tormented her. Basically, all she wants at this moment is a few weeks of tranquil, comfortable bourgeois existence, which Reich can obviously not offer her here in Moscow. As a matter of fact, I had not noticed her anxiety. It would only strike me the following day.

December 27. Asja's room in the sanatorium. We are there virtually every day from four to seven. Usually around five a female patient in one of the next rooms starts busying herself with zither music for an hour or half an hour. Sad chords are all she manages to produce. Music does not suit these bare walls very well. But the monotonous strumming doesn't seem to bother Asja. When we arrive, she is usually lying on the bed. Across from her on a small table there is milk, bread, and a plate with sugar and eggs which Reich generally takes home with him. But today she gave him an egg for me and wrote *Benjamin* on it. Over her dress Asja wears a gray woolen sanatorium smock. In the more comfortable part of the room that is reserved for her use, there are in addition three unmatched chairs, among them the deep armchair I usually sit in as well as the night table with its magazines, books, medications, a small colored bowl that probably belongs to her, the cold cream that I brought her from Berlin, a hand mirror that I once gave her; and for a long time Stone's design for the jacket of *One-Way Street* was also lying there. Asja often works on the blouse she is making for herself, pulling threads from a piece of fabric. — Light sources of the Moscow streets. As follows: the snow reflecting the lighting so brilliantly that almost all the streets are brightly illuminated, the powerful carbide lamps in the stalls of vendors, and the headlights of automobiles casting their beams hundreds of meters ahead in the street. In other major cities these headlights are forbidden: here, it is hard to imagine anything more irritating than this insolent evidence of the small number of vehicles at the disposition of a few NEP people (and certainly also the government bigwigs) that surmount the overall difficulty of moving from place to place. — Nothing very important to note about the day. Morning spent working at home. After lunch, I played chess with Reich; he took me in two matches. Asja was in the worst possible mood; I had never before witnessed such clear evidence of that nasty prickliness of hers which must make her so convincing in the role of Hedda Gabler. She would not even tolerate the slightest inquiry as to her health. There was finally no other alternative but to leave her alone. Our hope — Reich's and mine — that she would eventually join us at dominos was disappointed. Each time someone came into the recreation room, we turned and looked for her in vain. After the game we went back to her room, but I soon withdrew back to the recreation room with a book and it was only shortly before seven that I reappeared. Asja sent me on my way in a very unfriendly fashion, but then later she dispatched an egg to me via Reich on which she had written *Benjamin.* We had only been back in my room for a short while when she appeared. A swing of mood had taken place, she was seeing everything in a better light again, and was truly contrite about her behavior that afternoon. But all in all, when I look back over the recent weeks, I realize that her recovery, at least as far as her nerves are concerned, has barely progressed since my arrival. — In the evening Reich and I had a long conversation about my work as a writer and about the future direction it should take. He was of the opinion that I tended to belabor the things I was writing. In this same context he made the very pertinent observation that in great writing the proportion between the total number of sentences and those sentences whose formulation was especially striking or pregnant was about one to thirty — whereas it was more like one to two in my case. All this is correct. (As for the last point, this is probably still the aftereffect of Philipp Keller's[71] strong early influence on me.) But I did have to disagree with him when it came to certain ideas that have never been in doubt for me and that date all the way back to my early essay on "Language As Such and the Language of Man."[72] I referred him to the polarity that exists in every linguistic entity: to be at once expression and communication. This clearly related to something we had often discussed together, "the destruction of language" as a tendency of contemporary Russian literature. The development of the communicative aspect of language to the exclusion of all else in fact inevitably leads to the destruction of language. On the other hand, the way leads to mystical silence if its expressive character is raised to the absolute. Of the two, it seems to me that the more current tendency at the moment is toward communication. But in one form or another a compromise is always necessary. I did, however, concede that I was in a critical situation as far as my activity as an author was concerned. I told him that I saw no way out for myself here: mere convictions and abstract decisions were not enough, only concrete tasks and challenges could really help me make headway. Here he reminded me of my essays on cities.[73] This was most encouraging to me. I began thinking more confidently about a description of Moscow. To conclude things I read him my portrait of Karl Kraus,[74] since he had come up in the conversation.

December 28. I don't think there's another city with as many watchmakers as Moscow. This is all the more peculiar since people here do not get particularly worried about time. But there must be historical reasons for this. When you watch people on the street, you rarely see anybody rushing, unless it happens to be very cold. They have gotten in the habit of walking in zigzags. (It is quite significant that in some club or another, as Reich was telling me, there is a poster on the wall with the exhortation: Lenin said, "Time is Money." Just to express this banality, the highest authority had to be invoked.) I picked up my watch from the repair shop. — It was snowing in the morning and continued to do so off and on throughout the day. Later, a bit of a thaw set in. I understand how Asja used to miss the snow in Berlin, how the naked asphalt got to her.

71.   Benjamin knew Philipp Keller from his Freiburg student days (1913). Keller wrote a novel, *Gemischte Gefühle*, Leipzig, Kurt Wolff, 1913, and published in expressionist magazines.
72.   Written in 1916, posthumously published; included in *Reflections*, pp. 314–332.
73.   See "Naples," *GS*, IV, pp. 307–316, written together with Lacis, and Benjamin's later city portraits, for example those on Weimar, Marseilles, and San Gimignano.
74.   Included in *Einbahnstrasse*, but not among the selections translated in *Reflections*.

Winter here, like a peasant in a white sheepskin coat, advances under a thick fur of snow. — We got up late in the morning and then went to visit Reich's room. As an example of petit-bourgeois domesticity, it would be hard to imagine a more horrid specimen. The sight of hundreds of slipcovers, consoles, upholstered furniture, drapes is nearly enough to suffocate you; the air must be thick with dust. There was a tall Christmas tree in the corner by the window, and even it was ugly with its scraggly branches and the misshapen snowman at its crown. The tiring walk from the streetcar stop and the horror of this room clouded my overall perspective on the situation, and I agreed somewhat too hastily to Reich's proposal that I move in with him here in January. These petit-bourgeois interiors are the battlefields over which the devastating assault of commodity capital has victoriously swept, and nothing human can thrive here any more. But given my penchant for cave dwelling, perhaps I might just get a great deal of work done in this room. What remains to be decided, however, is whether I should give up the excellent strategic position of my current lodgings or hold on to them, even at the risk of losing out on the daily contact with Reich that provides me with so much vital information. Then we took a long walk through the streets of the suburbs: I had been promised a tour of a factory which specialized in the manufacture of tree decorations. The "prairie of architecture," as Reich had called Moscow, is even more of a wilderness in these streets than in the center of town. On both sides of the broad avenues, huts in the style of wooden peasant houses alternate with art-nouveau villas or the sober facades of six-story buildings. The snow lay deep and when silence suddenly fell, one could almost have believed oneself in a village in midwinter, deep in the hinterlands of Russia. Behind a row of trees stood a church with domes of blue and gold and, as always, with grates over the windows facing the street. The churches here often bear images of saints on their facades, such as one sees in Italy only on the most ancient churches (e.g., Sto. Freginiano in Lucca).[75] As it turned out, the woman who worked in the factory was not there, so we were unable to visit it. We soon went our separate ways. I went down to the Kusnetzky most [Ironworkers' bridge] to look at bookstores. Moscow's largest bookstore (to judge from its appearance) is located on this street. I even saw foreign literature in the windows, but at outlandish prices. Russian books, almost without exception, are sold unbound. Paper is three times as expensive here as in Germany, and is an import item for the most part, so they cut corners on appearances, or so it seemed to me. Along the way, I bought — having changed money at the bank — one of those hot pastry rolls you find everywhere on the streets here. After a few steps, a young boy lunged toward me, and when I had finally figured out that it was not money but bread he was after, I gave him a piece. — At noon I beat Reich at chess. The afternoon at Asja's, things just as wan as they had been for the past few days, Asja blunted

75.   San Frediano, built between 1112–1147.

by anxieties. I committed the grave error of trying to take Reich's defense against her absurd reproaches. He subsequently told me the following day that he wanted to go visit her on his own. That evening, by contrast, he seemed to want to be the best of friends. It had gotten too late to go to the dress rehearsal of Illés's play as we had planned, and since Asja was no longer coming, we went to attend the "legal proceedings" at the Krestiansky Club.[76] It was eight-thirty by the time we got there and we discovered that things had already started an hour ago. The hall was full and no more people were being admitted. But a shrewd woman turned my presence to her advantage. Realizing that I was a foreigner, she presented Reich and me as two visiting dignitaries she was escorting and so managed to get us all in. We entered a hall draped in red in which there were some three hundred people. It was filled to capacity, many people were standing. A bust of Lenin in a niche. The proceedings were taking place on the stage platform, flanked on the right and left by two painted proletarian figures, a peasant and a factory worker. Above the stage proscenium, the Soviet emblem. The hearing of evidence had already taken place by the time we arrived, an expert was now testifying. He sat at a small table with his assistant, opposite the table of the defense attorney, both facing sideways on the stage. The college of judges occupied a table that faced the public directly, in front of which sat the accused, a peasant woman dressed in black, holding a thick stick in her hands. All the participants were well-dressed. The peasant woman stood accused of illegal medical practice with fatal consequences. She had assisted at a birth (or an abortion), and some error on her part had brought about the unfortunate result. The lines of argument adduced in this case were extremely crude. The expert's testimony maintained: the death of the woman was directly attributable to the medical interference of the defendant. The defense pleaded: there was no evil intention, sanitary measures and medical expertise were not available in her part of the country. The prosecution demanded the death penalty. The peasant woman's summation: people always die. Then the presiding judge turned to the assembly: any questions? A Komsomol appeared on stage and made a plea for the harshest possible punishment. Then the court retired for deliberation — a pause ensued. Everybody stood to hear the verdict read. Two years' imprisonment with recognition of mitigating circumstances. Solitary confinement is thus ruled out. The presiding judge concluded by pointing out the necessity of establishing centers for medical care and education in rural areas. Everybody then dispersed. This was the first time in Moscow that I had seen such simple people at a gathering. There were probably many peasants among them, since this club is above all set up for peasants. I was taken on a tour of the premises. I was struck by the fact that the walls of the reading room were entirely covered with visual aids, just like the children's sanatorium. The material here consisted largely of statistics, some of which had

76.   Peasants' Club, on Trubnaia Square.

been illustrated with little color pictures, posted here by the peasants themselves (village life, agricultural development, production conditions, and cultural institutions were all recorded), but the walls are also covered with displays of tools, machine parts, chemical retorts, etc. Intrigued, I approached a shelf from which two African masks were grimacing down at me. But on closer inspection they turned out to be gas masks. Finally I was shown the club's dormitory. It is set up for peasant men and women, individuals and groups who are in the city on a *kommandirovka* [assignment]. The large rooms contain at most six beds; everybody puts their clothes on their bed for the night. The washrooms must be located somewhere else. The rooms themselves have no wash facilities. There are pictures of Lenin, Kalinin, Rykov, etc. on the walls. The cult of Lenin's image in particular is taken to incredible lengths here. There is a store on the Kusnetzky most that specializes in Lenin, and he comes in every size, pose, and material. In the club's common room, where a radio concert could be heard, there is a very expressive image of him in relief, depicting him as an orator, life-size, from the torso up. A more modest little picture of him graces the kitchens, laundries, etc. of most public institutes. The building has space for over four hundred guests. Under the increasingly oppressive escort of the guide who had initially gotten us in, we departed and decided, once we were finally alone again, to stop in at some *pivnaia* [alehouse] that was featuring evening entertainment. As we were entering, there were a few people at the door struggling to cart off a drunk. The room was not that large or crowded, and people were sitting alone or in small groups over beers. We took seats fairly close to the plank stage, whose backdrop consisted of a charming blur of meadow with a hint of a ruin that seemed to be dissolving into air. Still, this vista was not enough to cover the entire length of the stage. After two song numbers, the main attraction of the evening began — it was an *intsenirovka*, i.e., material adapted for the stage from other sources, such as epic or lyric. In this case the dramatic framework seemed to serve as a pretext for a medley of love songs and peasant songs. First a woman appeared on stage alone and listened for a bird. Then a man entered from the wings and it went on like this until the entire stage was full and everything ended in a chorus of song and dance. The whole thing did not differ all that much from a family festivity, but since such occasions are gradually disappearing from real life, they are probably all the more alluring to the petit bourgeois when they occur on stage. Odd what they serve with the beer: little bits of white bread or black bread with a crust of salt baked onto them, and dried peas in brine.

December 29. Russia is beginning to take on shape for the man on the street. A major propaganda film, *One-Sixth of the World*,[77] has been announced. On the

77.   *Shestaia chast mira*, commissioned by Gostorg, the Bureau of Trade, directed by Dziga

street in the snow lie maps of the SSR, piled up there by street vendors who offer them for sale. Meyerhold uses a map in *Daioch Evropu*[78] — on which the West is a complex system of small Russian peninsulas. The map is almost as close to becoming the center of a new Russian icon cult as is Lenin's portrait. Meanwhile the older practice continues in the churches. As I was walking around during the day, I entered the church of Our Lady of Kazan, which Asja had told me was one of her favorites. It is located in a corner of Red Square. First you enter into a spacious anteroom with a few scattered pictures of saints. It seems to be primarily at the disposal of the woman who looks after the church. It is gloomy; its half-light lends itself to conspiracies. In rooms like this, one can hatch the shadiest deals, even pogroms, should the occasion arise. Adjoining this room is the actual place of worship. It has a few small stairs in the background that lead up to the narrow, low platform on which one advances past the pictures of saints. Altar upon altar follows in close succession, each one indicated by the glimmer of a small red lamp. The lateral walls are taken up by very large pictures of saints. Those portions of the wall that are not hidden by pictures are covered in luminous gold. A crystal chandelier hangs from the cloying, painted ceiling. I observed the ceremony from a seat near the entrance. It involves the traditional adoration of images. One greets the large pictures by crossing oneself, then one falls to one's knees, touches one's forehead to the ground, and, after having again crossed himself, the worshipper or penitant proceeds on to the next. Before the small glass-covered pictures that lie on stands either singly or in rows, the genuflection is omitted; one bows over and kisses the glass. I approached them and noticed that next to the priceless ancient icons were to be found, on the very same stand, worthless, mass-produced chromolithographs. Moscow has many more churches than one initially suspects. The Western European locates them by their towers, high in the air. It takes practice to convert the long walls and masses of low domes into an extensive complex of cloister churches or chapels. Then it also grows clear why in certain spots Moscow looks as tightly packed as a fortress: low towers in the West are the distinguishing features of secular architecture. I was coming from the post office, had then sent a telegraph, and after a long roundabout search through the Polytechnical Museum,[79] I had been unable to find the exhibit of drawings by the mentally ill. To compensate myself, I took a walk down the stalls that run along the Kitai gorod wall. This is the center of the old book trade. It would be futile to try to track down any finds here in non-Russian lit-

---

Vertov (1896–1954), was first shown in Moscow on December 31, 1926. It presented a panoramic view of the breadth and ethnic variety of the U.S.S.R., contrasting its fraternal union with colonial exploitation under Western capitalism.
78.   *Europe is Ours (D.E.)*, a play by M. Podgaetsky, adapted from Ilya Ehrenburg's *Trust D.E.* and B. Kellermann's *The Tunnel*. First produced by Meyerhold on June 15, 1924.
79.   Center of the Federal Association for the Promotion of Political and Scientific Knowledge; many of Mayakovsky's literary events took place here.

Booksellers at the Kitai gorod wall.

erature. Even the older Russian editions (to judge by the bindings) are hard to come by here. Still, in the recent course of years, countless libraries must have been dispersed. Perhaps only in Leningrad? And not in Moscow, where libraries were rarer? In one of the stalls in the Kitaiski proezd [Chinese quarter], I bought a harmonica for Stefan. — A few more words on the open air markets. All the Christmas items (tinsel, candles, candle holders, tree decorations, even trees) are still on sale after December 24th. I think until the second, religious celebration of Christmas. — Comparison of the prices in the stalls to those in the state stores. Bought the *Berliner Tageblatt* of November 20 and December 8. On the Kusnetzky most a boy banging tiny clay plates and bowls together in order to test their solidity. A strange vision on the Okhotny riad: women standing there holding in their open hands a single piece of raw meat on a bed of straw, or a chicken or something similar, and offering it to the passers-by. They are unlicensed vendors. They don't have the money to pay the concession fee for a stand, nor the time to wait in line to rent one for a day or week. When a militia man appears, they simply take their merchandise and run. — I remember nothing of the afternoon. In the evening went with Reich to a terrible film (with Ilyinsky)[80] not far from my hotel.

80.   Igor Vladimirovich Ilyinsky (b. 1901), known especially for his comic roles; he worked with Meyerhold from 1920–1935. He created the role of Bruno in *The Magnificent Cuckold* and the title role in *Bubus the Teacher*. After leaving the Meyerhold Theater, he worked at the Maly Theater.

December 30. The Christmas tree is still standing in my room. Little by little I manage to order the sounds that surround me. The overture begins in the early morning and introduces several leitmotifs: first the stamping on the stairway across from my room that leads down to the basement. Most likely employees coming to work. Then the telephone in the hallway starts up and continues virtually without intermission until one or two in the morning. The telephones are outstanding in Moscow, far better than in Berlin or Paris. It only takes three or four seconds to put a call through. I quite frequently hear a loud child's voice talking into the telephone. Listening to the many digits, the ear grows familiar with Russian numerals. Then a man comes by around nine, and knocks on door after door to check if the trap window has been shut. This is when they start heating. Reich maintains that even when the window is closed, small amounts of coal gas seep into the room. This is certainly possible, considering how stuffy it is at night. In addition, heat is cast up from the floor, which, like volcanic ground, has its hot spots here and there. While you're still in bed, your sleep is shaken by a rhythmic thumping, as if huge steaks were being pounded; they're splitting wood in the courtyard. And despite all of this my room exudes tranquility. I have never lived in a room where it was this easy to work. — Some notes on Russia's situation. In conversations with Reich I have been insisting on how contradictory the current situation of Russia is. In its foreign policy the government is pursuing peace in order to enter into commercial treaties with imperialist states; domestically, however, it is above all trying to bring about a suspension of militant communism, to usher in a period free of class conflict, to de-politicize the life of its citizens as much as possible. On the other hand, its youth is being put through "revolutionary" education in pioneer organizations, in the Komsomol, which means that they do not come to revolution as an experience but only as a discourse. An attempt is being made to arrest the dynamic of revolutionary progress in the life of the state — one has entered, like it or not, a period of restoration while nonetheless wanting to store up the revolutionary energy of the youth like electricity in a battery. It doesn't work. Pride in communism, for which there is already a special word in Russian, has to be instilled in young people, who are often the first generation to have received more than a scanty education. The extraordinary difficulties of the restoration are also very evident in the problem of education. In order to combat the catastrophic lack of education, it has been decreed that knowledge of Russian and West European classics should be spread. (Parenthetically, this is why so much importance was accorded to Meyerhold's adaptation of *The Inspector General*, and to its failure.) And you can measure just how necessary this decree is when you learn that in a recent debate with Reich about Shakespeare, Lebedinsky[81] maintained that

81.   Yuri Lebedinsky (1898–1959). Known above all for his novels *Nedelia (A Week,* 1922) and *Kommisary (The Commissars,* 1925), both of which dealt with internal aspects of the Communist Party. He was active in the leadership of a number of associations of proletarian writers, including the VAPP.

he had lived before the invention of printing. From another perspective: these bourgeois cultural values have themselves entered into an extremely critical phase with the decline of bourgeois society. Given the way they present themselves today, given the shape they have taken over the past century in the hands of the bourgeoisie, they cannot be expropriated without in the process forfeiting the importance they have in the end acquired, however questionable or even deleterious this might be. These values, like precious glass, will have to undergo a long haul, one they will never survive without proper packaging. But to package is to render invisible, which goes counter to the Party's official promotion of the popularization of these values. It is now becoming evident in Soviet Russia that these values are being popularized in precisely the bleak, distorted guise for which, in the end, imperialism is to be thanked. A man like Walzel[82] is made a member of the academy and its president, Kogan, writes an article on Western literature in *Vecherniaia Moskva* that makes arbitrary and totally ignorant connections (Proust and Bronnen!)[83] and attempts, with a mere handful of names, to "inform" its readers about foreign writing. But probably the only cultural scene in the West to which Russia brings an understanding lively enough to be worth arguing about is that of America. Cultural entente as such, that is, not founded on concrete commercial ties, is a ploy of the pacifist variety of imperialism and for Russia it is a phenomenon of the restoration. Furthermore, access to information is considerably hampered by Russia's isolation from other countries. To put it more precisely: contact with the outside world is essentially routed through the Party and primarily involves political questions. The upper middle class has been destroyed; the newly created petite bourgeoisie is not materially or spiritually in a position to establish ties with the outside. At the present, a visa to travel abroad, if the trip is not taken under state or Party auspices, costs 200 rubles. Without a doubt Russia knows less about the rest of the world than the world (with the exception of the Latin countries) knows about Russia. The first and foremost concern here is to establish contacts among the various nationalities within the country's extraordinarily vast territory, and especially to establish contacts between peasants and workers. One could say that Russia's ignorance of the rest of the world is very much like the *chervonets* [ten rubles]: money that is very valuable in Russia but not recognized as currency abroad. It is extremely significant that a very run-of-the-mill Russian film actor, Ilyinsky, an unscrupulous, inept imitator of Chaplin, is considered a major comic here simply because Chaplin's films are so expensive that one

82.   Oskar Walzel (1864–1959), literary historian. An honorary member of the Soviet Academy, he was offered the Goethe article for the *Soviet Encyclopedia* after Benjamin's was rejected. (See Lunatcharsky's letter reproduced in the appendix.)
83.   Arnolt Bronnen (1895–1959), writer, theater director, and later critic. He became known in 1922 with his play *Vatermord* (*Patricide*), for which Brecht wrote the producer's directions. Bronnen had moved rapidly to the right by 1925; after World War II, he was a communist mayor and theater critic.

doesn't get to see them here.[84] Indeed, as a rule the Russian government does not invest much in foreign films. It counts on the competition between rival film industries which are out to conquer the Russian market and it buys cheap, acquiring films virtually for nothing, more or less as advertising samples or promotion items. Russian film itself, apart from a few outstanding productions, is not all that good on the average. It is fighting for subject matter. Film censorship is in fact very strict; quite unlike theater censorship, it circumscribes the area of subject matter, probably taking foreign distribution into consideration. A serious critique of Soviet man is impossible in film, which is not the case with theater. But the representation of bourgeois life is likewise impossible. And there is equally little room for American grotesque comedy, since it is based on uninhibited play with technique. But everything technical is sacred here, nothing is taken more earnestly than technique. Above all, however, Russian film knows nothing of eroticism. As is well known, the "bagatellization" of love and sex life is part and parcel of the communist credo. It would be considered counterrevolutionary propaganda to represent tragic love entanglements on film or stage. There remains the possibility of social comedy whose satirical target would essentially be the new bourgeoisie. Whether film, one of the most advanced machines for the imperialist domination of the masses, can be expropriated on this basis, that is very much the question. // Worked in the morning, then went with Reich to Gosfilm. But Pansky wasn't around. We all drove to the Polytechnical Museum. The entrance to the exhibit of pictures by the mentally ill turned out to be on a side street. The exhibit itself was only of mediocre interest; the material was almost without exception artistically uninteresting, but well presented and certainly of scientific value. A small guided tour was taking place while we were there: one learned only what had already been recorded on the small cards that accompanied each of the items on exhibit.

Reich then went on to Dom Herzena, and I followed after, having first stopped at the Institute to pick up tickets for the performance at Tairov's that evening. The afternoon at Asja's was again monotonous. In the sanatorium Reich managed to borrow (from the Ukrainian) a fur coat for the following day. We got to the theater on time. They were performing *Desire Under the Elms* by O'Neill.[85] The production was very poor, and Koonen[86] was especially disappointing, completely uninteresting. What was interesting (but as Reich correctly pointed out, erroneous) was the fragmentation of the play into single scenes (cinematization) by means of curtain falls and lighting changes. The tempo was far more rapid than is usually the case here and was further acceler-

84.   Benjamin's dismissal of Ilyinsky's work suggests that he was uninformed of the importance of the actor's role in the renewal of theatrical practice under Meyerhold.
85.   The première of O'Neill's play, staged by Tairov, took place at the Kamerny Theater in November 1926.
86.   Alicia Koonen (1889–1974), born in Belgium, a former member of Stanislavsky's MKHAT, married to Tairov.

ated by the dynamism of the decor. The set consisted of a cross-section view of
three rooms: on the ground floor, a large room with a view to the exterior and
an exit. At certain points, one saw its walls slide up at an 180-degree angle and
the outdoors seemed to stream in from every side. There were two more rooms
on the second floor, reached by a stairway that was partitioned off from the audience's view by laths. It was fascinating to follow the characters making their
way up and down the stairs behind this lattice. There are six headings on the
asbestos curtain advertising the program for the coming week (the theater is
closed Mondays). At Reich's request, I spent the night on the sofa and promised to wake him in the morning.

December 31. Reich drove out to visit Daga today. Asja came by around ten (I
wasn't ready yet) and we went to her seamstress. The entire outing was dull and
drab. It began with her reproaches: I was dragging Reich along with me everywhere and tiring him out. Later she admitted that she had been furious with
me all day because of the silk blouse I had brought her. It had ripped the very
first time she put it on. Stupidly, I added that I had bought it at Wertheim's.[87]
(A white lie — but stupid nonetheless.) Besides, it was all the more difficult for
me to say anything because the continual waiting for news from Berlin had already begun to wear me down. Finally we sat down in a cafe for a few minutes.
But it was almost as if we hadn't. Asja was thinking of only one thing: getting
back to the sanatorium on time. I have no idea why it should be that of late all
the life has been drained from the time we spend together and the looks we exchange. But my unsettled state makes it impossible to hide the fact. And to
swear Asja the undivided attention she demands is something I cannot do in
the absence of any encouragement or friendliness on her part. She herself is far-
ing poorly on account of Daga; the news Reich brought back about her did not,
to say the least, put her mind at ease. I am considering curtailing my afternoon
visits to her. Even her little room I find oppressive, for there are now usually no
less than three and often four people present, and even more when her roommate has visitors: I hear a lot of Russian, understand nothing, doze off or read.
I brought over some cakes to Asja in the afternoon. All she did was get irritated, she was in the worst possible mood. Reich had been to see her half an
hour previously (I had wanted to finish up a letter to Hessel)[88] and what he had
told her about Daga had considerably agitated her. Things were quite somber

87.   Major Berlin department store.
88.   Franz Hessel (1880–1941). Hessel was editor in chief at Rowohlt, publisher of Benjamin's
Einbahnstrasse and *Ursprung des deutschen Trauerspiels*. Benjamin met Hessel in 1922 and published
some of his Baudelaire translations in Hessel's short-lived magazine *Vers und Prosa*. Benjamin
pays handsome tribute to Hessel's *Nachfeier* (*Celebration*) at the outset of "A Berlin Chronicle,"
Reflections, pp. 7–9; at various times he reviewed four of Hessel's other books. See note 60 for
Hessel and Benjamin's collaborative translations of Proust.

for the entire time. I left early to go to the Meyerhold Theater to pick up tickets for the two of us for that night's performance of *Daioch Evropu*. Stopped by at the hotel for a moment to report that the show would begin at quarter of eight. In the process I checked for mail: there was none. At noon Reich had put me in touch with Meyerhold, who had promised me tickets. With great difficulty, I fought my way to the assistant director in order to pick them up. Much to my surprise, Asja arrived on time. She was again wearing her yellow shawl. Her face has an uncanny sheen to it these days. As we were standing in front of a poster before the performance began, I said to her: "You know, Reich is a fabulous guy." — "?" — "If I had to be sitting alone somewhere tonight, I would hang myself out of sheer misery." But even these words failed to liven up our conversation. The revue was quite interesting, and for a moment — I no longer exactly remember at what point it was — we again felt closer to each other. Now I remember — it was the "Café Riche" scene with the music and the Apache dances. "It's been fifteen years," I said to Asja, "that this Apache romanticism has been sweeping Europe and people fall for it every time." We spoke with Meyerhold in the intermissions. During the second one, he had a woman escort us to the "museum" where the models of his stage sets are preserved. There I saw the remarkable set for *Le cocu magnifique*,[89] the celebrated decor of *Bubus*,[90] with its bamboo enclosure (the various entrances and exits of the actors as well as all the high points of the play are accompanied by a louder or softer pounding of the poles), the ship's prow from *Rychi Kitai*,[91] with the water toward the front of the stage, and other things as well. I signed the guest register. In the final act, Asja was disturbed by the shooting. During the first intermission, as we were looking for Meyerhold (we only located him at the very end of the intermission), I was ahead of Asja on the stairs for a moment. Suddenly I felt her hand on my neck. My coat collar had gotten turned up and she was folding it back into place. At this contact I realized just how long it had been since any hand had touched me with gentleness. By eleven-thirty we were back on the street. Asja scolded me for not having purchased anything; otherwise, she said, she would have continued on to my place to celebrate New Year's Eve. I proposed that we go to a cafe, but to no avail. Nor would she accept the possibility that Reich might have bought something to eat. I accompanied her home, saddened and silent. The snow that night had the sparkle of stars. (On another occasion, I saw snow crystals on her coat such as probably never occur in Germany.) When we arrived in front of her house, I asked her, more out of defi-

89.   The sets and costumes for Meyerhold's production of Fernand Crommelynck's *Le cocu magnifique* (*The Magnificent Cuckold*) were designed by the constructivist artist Liubov S. Popova (1889–1924).

90.   The sets for A. Faikos's *Uchitel Bubus* (*Bubus the Teacher*) were designed by E. Shlepanov and Meyerhold. The play premiered on January 29, 1925.

91.   *Roar, China!* by Sergei Tretiakov, sets by Sergei Efimenko, directed by Meyerhold's pupil V. Fedrov. Shortly after the premiere on November 23, 1926, Meyerhold took over as director.

ance and more to test her than out of any real feeling, for one last kiss in the old year. She wouldn't give me one. I turned back, it was now almost New Year's, certainly alone but not all that sad. After all, I knew that Asja, too, was alone. A bell started ringing faintly just as I reached my hotel. I stood there for a while and listened. Reich was disappointed when he let me in. He had bought all sorts of things: port wine, halvah, lox, sausage. Now I was all the more upset that Asja had not come back to my place. But soon we were whiling away the time in lively conversation. And as I lay on the bed, I ate a great deal and took some good swigs of the port, so much so that in the end I was keeping up the conversation only mechanically and with considerable effort.

January 1. They're selling New Year's boughs on the street. Passing through Strasnoi Square I saw someone holding up long saplings with green, white, blue, and red paper blossoms glued onto them, every branch a different color. I would like to write on the "flowers" of Moscow, not dealing solely with the heroic Christmas roses but also with the huge hollyhocks on the lampshades which peddlers proudly brandish throughout the city. There are also tarts in the shape of cornucopias spilling forth cracker bonbons or pralines wrapped in different colors of paper. Cakes shaped like lyres. The "confectioner" of old children's literature seems to have survived only in Moscow. Only here can you find pictures created out of nothing more than spun sugar, sweet icicles on which the tongue takes its revenge against the bitter cold. One might also mention what the frost inspires, the peasant shawls whose designs, stitched in blue wool, imitate ice-flowers on the windowpane. The inventory of the streets is inexhaustible. Through the optician's eyeglasses I noticed the evening sky suddenly take on a southerly tint. Then the wide sleds with three bins for peanuts, hazelnuts, and *semechki* (sunflower seeds which, following a decree by the Soviet, are no longer allowed to be sold in public places). Then I saw a man who was selling small skates for dolls. Finally the tin trash cans — littering the streets is forbidden. Further notes on the shop signs: a few in Roman alphabet — Cafe, Tailleur. Every tap-room bearing the sign: *Pivnaia* — painted on a background whose upper border of drab green gradually shades off into a smudgy yellow. Many of the shop signs hang into the street at right angles. — I lingered in bed on New Year's morning. Reich didn't sleep late. We must have talked for over two hours. I can't remember exactly what about. We went out around noon. Finding the cellar restaurant where we usually eat on holidays closed, we went to the Hotel Liverpool. It was extraordinarily cold that day, I was proceeding with difficulty. I had a good corner seat at the table, a window to my right looking out on a courtyard full of snow. I have now adjusted to going without drink at my meal. We ordered the short menu. It was unfortunately served too quickly, I would have liked to have sat there a bit longer in the wood-paneled room with its few tables. There was not a single woman in the establishment. I found this quite soothing. I notice how the great need for calm that has come over me now that I have been delivered from my agonizing dependence on Asja discovers ever new wellsprings of tranquility. And of course, food and drink above all. Even the idea of my long journey back has acquired a soothing effect on me (as long as worries about household matters do not creep in as they have these past few days), the idea of reading a detective story (which I rarely do anymore, but I am playing with the thought), and the daily game of dominos at the sanatorium, which occasionally relieves the tension I feel with Asja. But today, insofar as I remember, there was no game. I asked Reich to purchase for me some tangerines which I was planning to give to Asja. I was not doing this because she had asked me the previous evening to bring her some the following day — I had even refused her request at that point — but rather because I was looking for a pretext to take a breather from our forced march through the cold. But Asja accepted the bag (on which, without telling her, I had written "Happy New Year") very sullenly (and my message went unnoticed). Evening at home, writing and talking. Reich began reading the baroque book.

January 2. I had a very hearty breakfast. Since we could not count on lunch, Reich had bought a number of things. Illés's play *Attentat* was to be performed for the press at one o'clock in the Theater of the Revolution. Misguidedly taking the public's thirst for the sensational into account, they had subtitled the play *Buy a Revolver*,[92] thereby giving away at the very outset the final twist in which the white guard assailant is discovered by the communists just as he is about to commit his deed, at which point he tries at least to palm his revolver off on them. The play contains an effective scene done in the style of Grand Guignol. It also has serious politico-theoretical ambitions, since it is supposedly meant to depict the hopeless situation of the petite bourgeoisie. But this was not conveyed at all by the production, given its lack of principles, its uncertainty, and its countless little winks at the audience. It even threw away its best trump cards, which were guaranteed by the suggestive settings — a concentration camp, a cafe, a barracks in the decaying, sordid, bleak Austria of 1919. I had never seen a more inconsistent handling of stage space: the entrances and exits were inevitably ineffectual. One could clearly observe what happens to Meyerhold's stagecraft when an incompetent director tries to appropriate it to his own purposes. The theater was packed. One could even see people wearing something like formal dress for the occasion. Illés was given a curtain call. It was very cold. I was wearing Reich's coat since for reasons of prestige he wanted to make a respectable impression at the theater. During the intermission we made the

92. *Kupite revolver*, directed by B. D. Koroleva, sets designed by S. Efimenko. The play premiered on December 30, 1926.

acquaintance of Gorodetsky[93] and his daughter. That afternoon at Asja's I happened into an interminable political discussion in which Reich was also participating. The Ukrainian and Asja's roommate were taking one side, she and Reich the other. The issue was once again opposition within the Party. But there was no possibility of reaching any understanding, not to mention any agreement, in this argument; the others were incapable of grasping the loss of prestige which, according to Asja and Reich, the Party would inevitably suffer should the opposition split off from it. It was only while smoking a cigarette downstairs with Reich that I would find out what the argument had been all about. All this talk in Russian among five people (a friend of Asja's roommate was also present), from which I was excluded, had again depressed and fatigued me. I was determined to leave should it continue. But when we got back upstairs, it was decided that we would play dominos. Reich and I teamed up against Asja and the Ukrainian. It was Sunday after New Year's Day. The "nice" nurse was on duty so we stayed on past dinner and played a few more combative rounds. I was feeling very good at the time, the Ukrainian had said he liked me a great deal. When we finally left, we stopped in a pastry shop for something warm to drink. When we got back home, there was a long conversation about my position as a free-lance writer, without party or profession. What Reich was saying to me was correct, I would have said the same thing to anybody who espoused the position I was taking. And I openly admitted this fact to him.

January 3. We set out early for the factory where Reich's landlady works. There was much to see; we spent some two hours there. To begin with, the Lenin niche. A whitewashed room, its rear wall draped in red, with red braid fringed with gold hanging from the ceiling. To the left, against this backdrop of red, stands the plaster bust of Lenin — as white as the whitewashed walls. A belt transmission projects into the room from the workshop where they manufacture tinsel next door. The wheel turns and the leather belts glide through a hole in the wall. The walls are hung with propaganda posters and portraits of famous revolutionaries or images that stenographically summarize the history of the Russian proletariat. The period of 1905–1907 is treated in the style of a huge picture postcard. It depicts, each overlapping the other, barricade battles, prison cells, the insurrection of the railway workers, the "Black Sunday" in front of the Winter Palace. Many of the posters are directed against alcoholism, a theme that is also addressed by the wall-newspaper which, according to the program, should appear every month but which in fact comes out somewhat less frequently. Its style on the whole resembles color comics for

93.   Sergei M. Gorodetsky (1884–1967), poet and librettist. He began as a symbolist poet, and helped found the Acmeists, of which he was a member from 1912–1921. He wrote for *Izvestia* until 1932.

children: pictures and prose with some poetry mixed in, all in various arrangements. But the newspaper serves above all to report the day-to-day events of
the collective that is gathered in this factory. Which is why it takes satirical
note of certain scandalous happenings, while also recording with statistical illustrations the educational progress that has been achieved of late. Other pla-
cards on the wall deal with hygiene: the use of gauze netting against flies is
recommended, the benefits of milk consumption are pointed out. About 150
people work here (in three shifts). The major products are: elastic bands,
spooled twine, string, silver cording, and Christmas tree decorations. It's the
only such factory in Moscow. But its structure is certainly less the result of "ver-
tical" organization than evidence of a primitive level of industrial specializa-
tion. Within a few meters of each other in the very same room, you can observe
the identical operation being performed by hand and by machine. To the right,
a machine rolls long strands of twine onto small spools, to the left a worker
cranks a large wooden wheel by hand: the identical process in both cases. The
majority of the employees are peasant women, and few of them belong to the
Party. They do not wear uniforms, they do not even wear work aprons, but sit
at their places as if they were doing domestic chores. In matronly fashion they
placidly bow over their task, their hair gathered under woolen babushkas. But
they are surrounded with posters warning against all the terrors of machine
operation. A worker is shown just as his arm is getting caught in the spokes of a
driving wheel, there is another one whose knee has gotten jammed between
two pistons, and a third one who has caused a short circuit by pushing the
wrong switch while drunk. The more delicate Christmas decorations are
manufactured entirely by hand. Three women sit in a brightly lit workshop.
One of them cuts the silvered threads down into small lengths, grabs a bundle
of them and then ties this together with a wire that slowly unwinds from a
spool. This wire travels through her teeth as if through a slot. Then she takes
the shiny bundles and teases them into star shapes and these are then passed
on to a coworker who glues a paper butterfly, or bird, or Father Christmas on
each of them. In another corner of the room sits a woman making stars out of
tinsel by a similar procedure, one per minute. As I bend over the wheel, she is
turning to observe her at work, she cannot stop laughing. Elsewhere they
manufacture silver piping, a product for the exotic regions of Russia, piping for
Persian turbans. (Downstairs the manufacture of tinsel: the man who shaves
the wire down with a whetstone. The strands of wire are reduced to two or
three hundredths of their diameter and then are silvered or sprayed with other
metallic colors. They are immediately transported to the uppermost story of the
building to be dried at high temperatures.) — Later I passed by the hiring hall.
Around noon food stands are set up at its entrance and sell hot cakes and fried
slices of sausage. From the factory we made our way over to Gnedin's.[94] He has

94.   Evgeny Gnedin (1898–1983), Soviet diplomat, presumed son of Alexandr Gelfand (Par-

long since lost the youthful looks he had two years ago, when I first met him that evening at the Russian embassy. But still clever and congenial. I was very careful in replying to his questions. Not only because people here are as a rule very sensitive and because Gnedin is particularly attached to communist ideas, but also because the only way to be taken seriously as an interlocutor here is to weigh every word with care. Gnedin is the advisor for central European affairs at the foreign ministry. His rather notable career (he has already turned down a more important position) is said to have something to do with the fact that he is the son of P. He was especially approving when I underscored the impossibility of comparing in detail the living conditions in Russia with those of Western Europe. I went to Petrovka to request a six-week extension of my visit. In the afternoon Reich wanted to go see Asja on his own. I therefore stayed home, ate something, and wrote. Reich returned around seven. We went to the Meyerhold Theater together where we met up with Asja. For Reich and Asja, the main event of the evening was the speech that Reich, at her request, was going to make in the course of the discussion. But things didn't turn out that way. Nonetheless he had to spend over two hours on the podium waiting among the circle of the other participants who had asked to speak. Sitting at a long green table were Lunacharsky, Pelche, the director of the artistic division of the Glav-Polit-Prosvet and president of the proceedings, Mayakovsky, Andrei Bely, Levidov, and many others.[95] In the first row of the orchestra seats sat Meyerhold himself. Asja left during the intermission and I accompanied her for a way since I could not follow the proceedings on my own. When I returned, a speaker from the opposition was declaiming with demogogic vehemence. But even though Meyerhold's opponents were in the majority among the audience, he was unable to win over the crowd. And when Meyerhold himself at least appeared, he was greeted with thunderous applause. But to his misfortune, he then proceeded to rely entirely on his oratorical temperament. What emerged was a display of rancor that repelled everybody. When he finally cast suspicions on one of his critics, claiming he had been attacked by him only because the critic had once worked for

---

vus). His memoirs, *Katastrophe und zweite Geburt*, appeared in Amsterdam in 1977.
95.   Anatoly Lunacharsky (1875–1922), writer and literary critic, People's Commissioner for Public Education. See his "Gogol-Meyerhold's *The Inspector General*," *October* 7, Winter 1978, pp. 57–70. Robert Pelche (1880–1955), communist journalist and art critic. Valerian Pletnyov (1886–1942), president of the central committee of the Federal Council of the Proletkult, became director in 1921 of the General Committee for Political Education (Glav-Polit-Prosvet). Vladimir Mayakovsky (1893–1930); his speech at the Meyerhold debate is included in his collected works. Andrei Bely, pseudonym of Boris Nikolaievich Bugaev (1880–1934), poet, novelist, and critic; he taught a course on "The Literary World" in Meyerhold's workshop. Mikhail Levidov (1891–1941), writer and journalist. Also in attendance were S. Tretiakov, J. Grossman-Rashchin, A. Slonimsky, N. Volkonsky, and I. Aksyonov. *Pravda* covered the debate in its January 9, 1927 issue. Benjamin described this scenario in "Disputation bei Meyerhold," *GS*, IV, pp. 481–483.

Meyerhold and had had differences with his boss, all contact with the audience was lost. And when he pulled out his files and tried to make a number of concrete justifications for some of the disputed aspects of his production, his efforts were no longer able to help. Even as he spoke many people were leaving and even Reich saw that it would now be impossible for him to intervene, and before Meyerhold was finished he came to sit with me. When he had finally concluded, the applause was only scattered. Since nothing more or new could now follow, we didn't wait for the proceedings to continue, but left instead.

January 4. My appointment with Kogan was set for today. But Nieman called up in the morning to inform me that I should appear at the Institute at one-thirty, that there was going to be a tour of the Kremlin. I spent the morning at home. Five or six people were gathered at the Institute, all apparently British except for me. Following a rather unlikable guide, we proceeded to the Kremlin by foot. The pace was brisk, I had the greatest trouble keeping up; in the end, the group had to wait for me at the entrance to the Kremlin. The first thing that strikes you inside the walls are the exaggeratedly well-maintained exteriors of the government buildings. I can only compare it to the impression conveyed by the buildings in the small storybook principality of Monaco, whose residents are privileged by the closest proximity to their rulers. Even the light colors of the facades, painted in white or creamy yellow, are similar. But whereas everything there takes sides in the pitched play of light and shadow, here the uniform brightness of the snowfield dominates and the composure of colors is cooler against it. Later, when the light gradually began to wane, the field seemed to take on an even greater expanse. Just beyond the luminous windows of the administrative buildings, the towers and domes were rising against the night sky: defeated monuments standing guard at the victors' gates. Bundles of light beamed from car headlights racing through the dark. The horses of the cavalry, who have a large drill ground here in the Kremlin, shy in their light. Pedestrians steer a difficult course between the automobiles and the skittish horses. Long rows of sleighs used for carting off the snow, isolated horsemen. Silent flocks of ravens have settled on the snow. The guards at the Kremlin gate stand watch in the blinding light, outfitted in bold ochre furs. Above them shines the red light that regulates the traffic passing through the gate. All the colors of Moscow converge here prismatically, at the center of Russian power. The Red Army Club looks out on this expanse. We visited it before leaving the Kremlin. The rooms are bright and clean, they seem to be somewhat more simply and more austerely maintained than the other clubs. There are many chess tables in the reading room. Thanks to Lenin, who himself was a player, chess has been officially sanctioned in Russia. A wooden relief map hangs on the wall: a schematically simplified outline of Europe. If you turn the handle next to it, all the places Lenin ever lived in Russia and in

Lenin's tomb outside the Kremlin.

Europe light up one after another in chronological sequence. But the apparatus works poorly, many places light up at the same time. The club has a lending library. I was delighted by a poster that detailed in words and in pretty colored images how many ways there are to avoid ruining a book. The tour, in fact, was poorly organized. It was about two-thirty when we finally entered the Kremlin and when, after having visited the Oruchenaia Palata,[96] we at last arrived at the churches, it had gotten so dark that one could see nothing of their interiors. But their tiny windows are placed so high that additional illumination of the interior is required in any event. We visited two cathedrals: Archangel and Uspensky Cathedrals. The latter used to be the coronation church of the czars. Their power had to represent itself in its fullest expansion within these numerous, but extremely small spaces. The tension thereby generated in these ceremonies is difficult to imagine today. Here in the churches our tedious tour guide withdrew and congenial elderly custodians slowly lit up the walls with candles. Unfortunately, there was not much to see. Nor can the multitude

96.   The Kremlin arsenal, constructed between 1844–1851.

of images, all of which seem superficially to be identical, say much to the un-trained eye. Nonetheless it was still light enough to view the splendid churches from the exterior. I especially remember a gallery in the Grand Palace of the Kremlin densely covered with the gleaming colors of little domes; I believe it contained the apartments of the princesses. The Kremlin was once a forest — its most ancient chapel is called the Church of the Redeemer in the Forest.[97] Then it later became a forest of churches and even though the last czars cleared it out to make room for new buildings of no consequence, enough was still left over to form a labyrinth of churches. Here, too, many images of saints stand watch on the facades, looking down from the highest cornices like birds that have taken refuge under the tin eaves. Their heads, bowed like retorts, bespeak sorrow. Unfortunately most of the afternoon was devoted to visiting the enor-mous collections of the Oruchenaia Palata. Their splendor is dazzling, but they are a distraction when one is trying to focus all of one's energies on the ex-traordinary topography and architecture of the Kremlin. It is easy to overlook one of the basic conditions of its beauty: none of its broad expanses contains a monument. There is, by contrast, hardly a square in Europe whose secret structure was not profaned and impaired over the course of the nine-teenth century by the introduction of a monument. One item in the collections that particularly struck me was a carriage that Prince Razumovsky[98] had given as a present to one of Peter the Great's daughters. Its protuberant, undulating ornamentation would make anybody dizzy on terra firma, even before imagin-ing how it might pitch and toss once on the road; when you discover that it was brought from France by sea, the discomfort is complete. All these treasures were acquired in a manner that has no future. — Not only their style but also the very way in which they were acquired are now defunct. They must have been a burden to their final owners, and one can imagine that the awareness that these things were at their disposition could almost have made them lose their minds. But now a picture of Lenin hangs at the entrance to these collec-tions, as if converted heathens had planted a cross where sacrifices previously used to be made to the gods. — The remainder of the day went fairly poorly: lunch was out of the question, it was around four when I left the Kremlin. Then Asja had not yet returned from the seamstress when I dropped by. Only Reich and Asja's inescapable roommate were there. Reich, however, couldn't wait any longer and shortly thereafter Asja appeared. Unfortunately we even-tually got to talking about the baroque book, and she made her usual observa-tions. Then I read her something from *One-Way Street*. We had been invited out by Gorodinsky (?) that evening. But here again, as had happened earlier with Granovsky, we missed dinner. For just as we were about to leave, Asja arrived to have a few more words with Reich, and when we turned up at the appointed

97.   Sobor Spasa na boru, a chapel built in 1330.
98.   Andrei Kirillovich Razumovsky (1752–1836).

place one hour late, only his daughter was still there. There was nothing left to do with Reich that evening. We wandered around for a while looking for a restaurant so I could get a little bite to eat, but we landed in an extremely basic eating establishment with rough wooden partitions and then finally ended up in a disagreeable *pivnaia* near Lubianka with terrible food. Then half an hour at Illés's — he wasn't there, but his wife fixed us some outstanding tea — and then back home. I would have liked to have gone to see *One-Sixth of the World* at the cinema with Reich, but he was too tired.

January 5. Moscow is the most silent of great cities, and doubly so when there is snow. The principal instrument in the orchestra of the streets, the automobile horn, is rarely played here; there are few cars. Similarly, in comparison with other centers, there are very few newspapers, basically only one tabloid, the single evening paper that comes out around three every day. And finally the calls of the street vendors are also very subdued. The street trade is for the most part illegal and does not want to call attention to itself. So the vendors address the passers-by less with calls than with measured, if not whispered, words in which there is something of the pleading tone of beggars. Only one caste parades noisily through the streets here: the rag-and-bone men with their sacks

Two views of the Sukharevsky market.

on their backs; their melancholy cry traverses every Moscow street once or
several times a week. There is one thing curious about the streets: the Russian
village plays hide-and-seek in them. If you pass through any of the large gate-
ways — they often have wrought-iron gratings, but I never encountered one
that was locked — you find yourself at the threshold of a spacious settlement
whose layout is often so broad and so expansive that it seems as if space cost
nothing in this city. A farm or a village opens out before you. The ground is
uneven, children ride around in sleighs, shovel snow; sheds for wood, tools, or
coal fill the corners, there are trees here and there, primitive wooden stairs or
additions give the sides or backs of houses, which look quite urban from the
front, the appearance of Russian farm houses. The street thus takes on the
dimension of the landscape. — In fact, nowhere does Moscow really look like
the city it is, rather it more resembles the outskirts of itself. The soggy ground,
the wooden booths, the long convoys of raw materials, the cattle being driven
to slaughter, the shabby dives can all be found in the most central parts of
town. This became very clear to me as I was walking along Sukharevskaia
today. I wanted to see the famous Sukharev Park. With over a hundred booths,
it is the descendant of a great fair. I entered it via the quarter of the scrap-iron
dealers, which lies right next to the church (Nikolaievsky Cathedral) whose
blue domes rise above the market. The people simply lay their merchandise out

on the snow. One finds old locks, meter rulers, hand tools, kitchen utensils, electrical appliances, etc., etc. Repairs are also done on the spot; I saw something being soldered over a jet of flame. There are no seats anywhere, everybody just stands and gossips or trades. The market reaches all the way down to Sukharevskaia. As I walked through the numerous intersections and alleyways of booths, I became aware that this particular configuration of market and fairground was also characteristic of a good portion of Moscow's streets. You come across watchmaker or garment districts, or centers for electrical supplies and machine parts, and then entire stretches without a single store on the street. Here at the market, the architectonic function of merchandise becomes clear: cloth and fabric form buttresses and columns, shoes and *valenki* hanging in a row on a string above the counter become the roof of the booth, large *garmoshkias* [accordions] create walls of sound, Memnon walls as it were. It was here among the toy stalls that I also finally found my Christmas tree decoration in the shape of a samovar. It was the first time in Moscow that I had seen stands selling images of saints. Most of them are, in traditional fashion, covered with silver foil stamped with the folds of the robe of the Virgin. The only colored surfaces are her head and her hands. There are also small glass cases in which you can see the head of St. Joseph (?) decorated with shiny paper flowers. Then these same flowers, large bunches of them, out in the open. They are more brilliant against the snow than colorful blankets or raw meat. But since this branch of business belongs to the paper and picture trade, these booths selling images of saints are situated next to the stands that deal in paper articles, so that they are surrounded on every side by portraits of Lenin, like prisoners flanked by policemen. Christmas roses here as well. They alone have no assigned place and surface now among foodstuffs, now among textiles, now among table ware. But they outshine everything, raw meat, brightly colored blankets, and gleaming dishes. Toward Sukharevskaia the market thins out into a narrow passageway between walls. Children stand here selling household wares, cutlery, towels, etc.; I saw two standing by the wall singing. And it was here that for the first time since Naples I came across someone selling magic items. He had a small bottle in front of him in which a large cloth monkey was sitting. One could not figure out how it had gotten in there. In fact, all one had to do was place one of the little animals the man was selling into the bottle. The water would swell it up to size. A Neapolitan used to sell bunches of flowers of the same sort. I walked along Sadovaia a bit further and then went to see Basseches around twelve-thirty. He has much to say, some of which is instructive, but his constant repetitions and irrelevant pointers convey only his desire for recognition. But he is kind, and the information he gives me, the German magazines he loans me, the secretary he has arranged for me, are all useful. — I did not go right over to Asja's in the afternoon: Reich wanted to speak to her alone and asked me to come by at five-thirty. Of late I barely manage to speak to Asja anymore. First of all, her health had once again worsened considerably. She has a temperature. But this might make her more inclined to engage in quiet conversation, were it not for the fact that besides Reich's far more discreet company there is the paralyzing presence of her roommate, who talks with noisy animation, dominates every discussion, and — to top it off — understands so much German that she robs me of whatever energy I still have left. In one of our rare moments alone, Asja asked whether I would come back to Russia again. I told her not without some Russian. And then it depended on several other things as well, money, my condition, her letters. They would depend, she said evasively — but I know how evasive she almost always is — on her health. I left and returned with the tangerines and halvah she had requested, and left them with the nurse downstairs in the sanatorium. Reich wanted the use of my room for the evening to work with his translator. I couldn't make up my mind to go to *Den' i noch*[99] at Tairov's alone. I went to see *One-Sixth of the World* (at the Arbat cinema). But there was much that escaped me.

January 6. The previous day I had sent off a telegram for Dora's birthday in the afternoon. Then I walked the entire length of Miasnitskaia up to the Red Gate and turned into one of the broad lateral streets that fan out from there. It was during this walk, when it was already dark, that I discovered the landscape of Moscow courtyards. I had now been in Moscow for a month. The next day was uneventful, nothing much to note. As we were having coffee in the friendly little pastry shop, which I will probably often think back on, Reich gave me an analysis of the contents of the film program that I had picked up the previous evening. Then I went to do some dictation at Basseches's. He had placed an attractive, agreeable secretary at my disposal, exceptionally competent. But she costs three rubles an hour. Whether I'll be able to manage it, I don't yet know. After the dictation Basseches accompanied me to Dom Herzena. The three of us ate together. Reich immediately went to Asja's after the meal. I had to stay on for a bit with Basseches, and I even managed to make arrangements to go see *Storm*[100] with him the following evening. Finally he accompanied me back as far as the sanatorium. Things were bleak upstairs. Everybody threw themselves on the German magazines that I had been imprudent enough to bring along. In the end Asja made it clear that she wanted to go to the seamstress's and Reich announced that he was going to accompany her. I said "farewell" to Asja through the door and trundled off home. The hope that she might yet come visit me that evening was not realized.

99. *Day and Night*, staged by Tairov at the Kamerny Theater.
100. *Storm*, a play by Vladimir Bill-Belotserkovsky (1884–1970), staged by E. Liubimov-Lanskoi in 1925.

January 7. State capitalism in Russia retains many of the features of the inflation era. Above all the juridical uncertainties in domestic affairs. On the one
hand, NEP has been authorized, but on the other it is only tolerated in the
interest of the state. Any NEPman can, from one day to the next, fall victim to
a turnabout in economic policy or to a passing whim of propaganda. Nonetheless there are fortunes — and from the Russian point of view they are colos-
sal — accumulating in certain hands. I have heard of people who pay more
than 3,000,000 rubles in taxes. These citizens are the counterpart to the heroism of wartime communism, theirs is a heroism of NEPmanship.[101] For the
most part, these individuals find themselves launched in this direction quite in-
dependently of their own personal dispositions. For as concerns domestic
trade, the distinguishing feature of the NEP era is precisely that government
investment has been strictly limited to basic commodities. This creates a very
advantageous climate for the business dealings of the NEPman. Another feature of the inflation era are the ration cards, which alone enable one to purchase the variety of products in the state stores, hence the lines. The hard currency is stable, but the prices of many of the items on display are given in
coupons, so that paper continues to play a major role in business transactions.
Even the oblivious attitude toward clothing is something one only saw in
Western Europe during the inflation era. Admittedly the convention of not car-
ing how one dresses is beginning to be overturned. Once a uniform of the ruling class, it now threatens to become a sign of those who are weakest in the
struggle for existence. In the theaters, the first formal gowns are gingerly
emerging, like Noah's dove after all the weeks of rain. But people's appearance
is still quite uniform, quite proletarian: the typically Western European kinds
of headwear, the soft felt hat or the derby, have apparently disappeared completely. Most in evidence are Russian fur hats or sport caps, which are also
often worn by girls with attractive but provocative variations (with long pro-
truding visors). As a rule people don't take them off in public: also the tipping
of hats in greeting has become more casual. The other articles of clothing are
already governed by an Oriental diversity. Fur vests, velvet jackets, leather
jackets, urban elegance and village costumes are blended among the men and
women. Here and there, as in other big cities, one still encounters (among
women) peasant national costumes. — I spent most of the morning at home today. Then went to see Kogan, the president of the Academy. I was not surprised by his inconsequentiality; everybody had prepared me for it. I picked up
theater tickets at the Kameneva office. During the interminable wait, I leafed
through a book on the posters of the Russian Revolution with many outstanding illustrations, some of which were in color. It occurred to me that however
effective these posters might be, they contain nothing that couldn't be easily ex-
trapolated from the stylistic elements of bourgeois decorative art, and a not

---

101. A play on the German verb *neppen*, to diddle, to swindle — trans.

very advanced sort of art for that matter. I did not run into Reich at Dom Herzena. At Asja's, I initially found myself alone with her, she was very listless, or perhaps only pretending to be in order to avoid any conversation with me. Then Reich arrived. I left in order to make arrangements with Basseches for the theater that evening, and since I was unable to reach him by telephone, I had to go there myself. Headaches all afternoon. Later we went to *Storm* with his woman friend, an operetta singer. She seemed very shy and out of sorts and returned home immediately after the theater. *Storm* depicts episodes from the period of wartime communism, focused around a typhus epidemic in the countryside. Basseches generously translated for me and the acting was better than usual, so I got a great deal out of the evening. What the play lacks, as do all Russian plays (Reich), is a dramatic plot. It had, it seemed to me, the news interest of a decent chronicle, but this does not constitute dramatic interest. Around midnight I ate at the Kruzhok[102] on Tverskaia with Basseches. But since it was the first day of Christmas celebrations (old style), things were not all that lively in the club. The food was excellent: vodka flavored with an extract of herbs which colored it yellow and made it go down far more easily. Discussed the project for a report on French art and culture for the Russian newspapers.

January 8. Changed money in the morning and then dictated. The report on the debate at Meyerhold's may have turned out more or less well, but on the other hand I was not able to make any headway on the account of Moscow for the *Diary.* Early that morning there had been an altercation with Reich because I had (somewhat thoughtlessly) appeared at Dom Herzena with Basseches. Yet another lesson in how careful one has to be here. This is one of the most conspicuous symptoms of the thoroughgoing politicization of life. While dictating at the embassy I was relieved not to see Basseches, who was still in bed. In order not to have to go to Dom Herzena, I bought myself some caviar and ham and ate at home. When I arrived at Asja's at four-thirty, Reich was not yet there. It was another hour before he arrived and he later told me that he had again had a heart attack on the way over. Asja's condition had worsened and she was so self-involved that she barely noticed Reich's late arrival. She is again running a temperature. Her by now unbearable roommate was present nearly the entire time and even received a visitor herself later. In fact, she is usually quite friendly — it's just that she is always hovering around Asja. I read the project for the *Diary* and she made a number of pertinent observations. There was even a certain friendliness that developed over the course of the conversation. Then we played dominos in her room. Reich arrived. And then the four

102. The name refers to a term used in the 1840s signifying a small circle of young intellectuals gathered to discuss political and philosophical issues.

of us played. Reich had a meeting that evening. Around seven I had some coffee with him at our usual pastry shop, then I went home. It is becoming clearer and clearer to me that my work needs some sort of solid framework for the immediate future. Translation can obviously not provide this. In fact, this construction depends first and foremost on my taking a position. Only purely external considerations hold me back from joining the German Communist Party. This would seem to be the right moment now, one which it would be perhaps dangerous for me to let pass. For precisely because membership in the Party may very well only be an episode for me, it is not advisable to put it off any longer. But there are and there remain external considerations which force me to ask myself if I couldn't, through intensive work, concretely and economically consolidate a position as a left-wing outsider which would continue to grant me the possibility of producing extensively in what has so far been my sphere of work. Whether this production can move ahead into another phase without a break, that is the question. And even in this case, the "framework" would have to be propped up by external circumstances, an editorial position for example. At any rate, the period that lies ahead seems to me to distinguish itself from the previous one in that the erotic is becoming far less of a determining factor. My observation of Reich's and Asja's relation has, to a certain extent, made me more conscious of this. I note that Reich manages to weather all of Asja's ups and downs and is, or seems to be, rarely ruffled by patterns of behavior that would make me sick. And even if this is only an appearance, that's already a great deal. It's because of the "framework" he has found for his work here. In addition to all the actual contacts with which his work provides him, there is also the fact that he is a member of the ruling class here. It is precisely this transformation of an entire power structure that makes life here so extraordinarily meaningful. It is as insular and as eventful, as impoverished and yet in the same breath as full of possibilities as gold rush life in the Klondike. The dig for power goes on from early morning to late at night. The entire scheme of existence of the Western European intelligentsia is utterly impoverished in comparison to the countless constellations that offer themselves to an individual here in the space of a month. Admittedly this can lead to a certain state of inebriation in which it becomes almost impossible to conceive of a life without meetings and committees, debates, resolutions, and ballotings (all of which are the wars or at least the maneuvers of the will to power). But this [. . .] is the [precise goal][103] that so unconditionally forces one to take a position, that poses the dilemma as to whether one is going to remain in the hostile and exposed, uncomfortable and draughty spectator area, or whether one is going to adopt some sort of role in the commotion on stage.

103. Conjectural reading.

January 9. Further considerations: join the Party? Clear advantages: a solid position, a mandate, even if only by implication. Organized, guaranteed contact with other people. On the other hand: to be a Communist in a state where the proletariat rules means completely giving up your private independence. You leave the responsibility for organizing your own life up to the Party, as it were. But where the proletariat is oppressed, it means rallying to the oppressed class with all the consequences this might sooner or later entail. The seductiveness of the role of outrider — were it not for the existence of colleagues whose actions demonstrate to you at every occasion how dubious this position is. Within the Party: the enormous advantage of being able to project your own thoughts into something like a preestablished field of force. The admissibility of remaining outside the Party is in the final analysis determined by the question of whether or not one can adopt a marginal position to one's own tangible objective advantage without thereby going over to the side of the bourgeoisie or adversely affecting one's own work. Whether or not a concrete justification can be given for my future work, especially the scholarly work with its formal and metaphysical basis. What is "revolutionary" about its form, if indeed there is anything revolutionary about it. Whether or not my illegal incognito among bourgeois authors makes any sense. And whether, for the sake of my work, I should avoid certain extremes of "materialism" or seek to work out my disagreements with them within the Party. At issue are all the mental reservations inherent in the specialized work which I have undertaken so far. And the battle will only be resolved — at least experimentally — by joining the Party, should my work be unable to follow the rhythm of my convictions or organize my existence on this narrow base. As long as I continue to travel, joining the Party is obviously something fairly inconceivable. — It was Sunday. Translated all morning. Lunch in a small restaurant in Bolshaia Dimitrovka. The afternoon at Asja's; she was feeling very ill. Evening alone in my room, translating.

January 10. An extremely disagreeable argument with Reich took place this morning. He had decided to take me up on my proposal to read him my report on the debate at Meyerhold's.[104] I no longer had any desire to do so, but went ahead anyway with an instinctive reluctance. Given the previous conversations about my contributions to the *Literarische Welt*, nothing good could certainly come of it. So I read the thing quickly. But I was positioned so poorly on my chair, looking straight into the light, that this alone would have been enough for me to predict his reaction. Reich listened with a tense impassiveness, and when I had finished, limited himself to a few words. The tone in which he said them immediately touched off a quarrel that was all the more irresoluble

104. Published in the *Literarische Welt*, February 11, 1927, under the title "Der Regisseur Meyerhold—in Moskau erledigt?" Also in *GS*, IV, pp. 481–483.

because its actual grounds could no longer be mentioned. In the middle of the exchange there was a knock at the door — Asja appeared. She left again soon thereafter. While she was present I said very little: I worked at my translation. In a terrible frame of mind I went over to Basseches's to dictate some letters and an article. I find the secretary most agreeable, if somewhat ladylike. When I learned that she wanted to go back to Berlin, I gave her my card. I was not keen about running into Reich at lunch, so I bought myself some food and ate in my room. On my way over to Asja's I stopped for some coffee, and later, going back home after the visit, I had some more. Asja was feeling quite ill, got tired right away; I left her alone so she could get some sleep. But there were a few minutes during which we were alone in the room (or during which she acted as though we were). It was at that point that she said that when I again came to Moscow and she was well, I wouldn't have to wander around on my own so much. But if she didn't get well here, then she would come to Berlin; I would have to give her a corner of my room with a folding screen, and she would follow treatment with German doctors. I spent the evening alone at home. Reich arrived late and had a number of things to recount. But following the morning's incident, at least this much was clear to me: I could no longer count on Reich for whatever concerned my stay here, and if it could not be profitably organized without him, then the only reasonable thing to do would be to leave.

January 11. Asja again needs to get some injections. She wanted to go to the clinic today and it had been earlier arranged that she would stop by and fetch me so I could accompany her there by sleigh. But she didn't come by until around noon. They had already given her the injection at the sanatorium. She was as a result in a somewhat agitated state and when we were alone in the corridor (both she and I had telephone calls to make), she clung to my arm in a momentary access of her former boldness. Reich had taken up his position in the room and was making no signs of leaving. So that even though Asja had finally come to my room in the morning once again, it was totally pointless. I put off leaving for a number of minutes, but to no avail. She announced that she didn't want to accompany me. I therefore left her alone with Reich, went to Petrovka (but still was unable to obtain my passport) and then to the Museum of Painting. After this little episode, my mind was finally made up to fix the date of my departure, which in any case was rapidly approaching. There was not much to see in the museum. I learned later that Larionov and Goncharova[105] were big names. Their stuff is worthless. Just like most of the things

---

105. Mikhail Larionov (1881–1964) and Natalia Goncharova (1881–1962), avant-garde painters (rayonism, orphism, etc.), who from 1915–1929 collaborated on the set designs for Diaghilev's Russian ballets in France.

hanging in the three rooms, they seem to be massively influenced by Parisian and Berlin painting of the same period, which they copy without skill. — Around noon I spent hours in the Office of Culture waiting to get tickets for the Maly Theater[106] for Basseches, his woman friend, and myself. But since they were unable to inform the theater by telephone at the same time, our passes were not accepted that evening. Basseches had come without his friend. I would have liked to have gone to the cinema with him, but he wanted to eat and so I accompanied him to the Savoy. It is a far more modest establishment than the Bolshaia Moskovskaia.[107] I was also fairly bored with him. He is incapable of talking about anything other than his most private affairs; and when he does, it is with a visible awareness of how well-informed he is and how superbly capable he is of imparting this information to others. He continued to leaf through and read around in the *Rote Fahne*.[108] I accompanied him in the car for a stretch and then went straight home, where I did some more translating. — That morning I bought my first lacquer box (on Petrovka). It had been several days now that, as often happens with me, I had been concentrating exclusively on one thing as I made my way through the streets: it was lacquer boxes in this particular case. A short, passionate infatuation. I would like to buy three of them — but am not entirely sure how to allot the two acquired in the meantime. That day I bought the box with the two girls sitting by a samovar. It is quite beautiful — even though it has none of that pure black which is often the most beautiful thing about such lacquerwork.[109]

January 12. Today in the Kustarny Museum I bought a lacquer box on whose cover a female cigarette vendor is painted against the ground of black. A slender little tree stands next to her, and next to it, a boy. It is a winter scene, since there is snow on the ground. The box with the two girls also suggests snowy weather, for the room in which they are sitting has a window which seems to be filled with frosty blue air. But this is not certain. This new box was far more expensive. I chose it from a large selection that featured much that was ugly: Slavic copies of the Old Masters. Especially expensive are the boxes painted with gold (this must go back to older models), but I do not find them attractive. The motif on the larger box is certainly quite modern; the word *Mosselprom*[110] is visible on the vendor's apron. I know that I once saw similar boxes in a very elegant shop in the rue du Faubourg Saint-Honoré and that I stood

106. The little (national academic) theater (Maly Theatr).
107. The Savoy and the Bolshaia Moskovskaia were two famous Moscow hotels.
108. Journal of the German Spartacists, then a communist journal.
109. See Benjamin's essay on "Russian Toys," pp. 123–124 of this issue.
110. Moscow Association of Companies for the Transformation of Agricultural Products. Mayakovsky's and Rodchenko's publicity poetry for this enterprise contributed considerably to the fame of Mosselprom.

looking at them for a long time. But on that occasion I resisted the temptation to buy one; my idea was that I should receive one from Asja — or perhaps wait until I got to Moscow. This passion goes back to the powerful impression that one of these boxes always made on me in the apartment which Bloch shared with Else in Interlaken;[111] and from this I can imagine just how unforgettably these images on a ground of black lacquer must impress themselves on children. But I have forgotten the motif that decorated Bloch's box. — It was also today that I discovered some fabulous postcards, the kind I had long been looking for, old white elephants from the czarist days, primarily colored pictures on pressed cardboard, also views of Siberia (one of which I will use to try to mystify Ernst [Bloch]), etc. They were in a store on Tverskaia and since the owner spoke German, there was not the usual strain I feel when purchasing things here, so I took my time. I had gotten up and left the house early that morning. Then Asja had appeared around ten o'clock, finding Reich still in bed. She had stayed for half an hour, doing impressions of actors and imitating the singer who had composed "San Francisco," a cabaret song which she had apparently often heard him sing. I knew the song from Capri, she occasionally used to sing it there. I had initially hoped that I might accompany her in the morning and that we might go to a cafe together. But it was getting late. I left with her, put her on a streetcar, and then proceeded on alone. Her morning visit had a beneficial effect on the entire day. Admittedly, I was at first somewhat upset upon arriving at the Tretiakov Gallery. The two rooms which I had been most looking forward to seeing were closed. But the other rooms proved to be a pleasant surprise: I was able to walk around this museum as I had never previously been able to do in an unfamiliar collection, completely relaxed, giving myself over to the childish desire simply to observe what stories the pictures were telling. Half of the pictures in the museum are Russian genre paintings; its founder started collecting around 1830 (?) and had concentrated almost exclusively on contemporary artists. Later the horizon of his collection was extended to 1900 or thereabouts. And since, with the exception of the icons, the earliest things seem to date from the second half of the eighteenth century, this museum therefore provides an overview of the history of Russian art in the nineteenth century, a period in which genre paintings and landscapes predominated. What I saw leads me to conclude that of all the European nations, the Russians developed genre painting the most intensively. And these walls full of narrative paintings, representations of scenes from all walks of life, transform the gallery into a vast picture book. There were in fact far more visitors here than in the other collections I had seen. To watch them move through the rooms, in groups, sometimes with a guide or standing all alone, is to realize how at ease they are, how free they are of that dour intimidation that one observes among those rare proletarians that visit Western museums: first

111. Ernst Bloch (1885–1977) lived with his wife Else Bloch von Stritzki (1882–1921) in Interlaken, Switzerland, from 1917–1919.

of all, because the proletariat here has truly begun to take possession of the cultural resources of the bourgeoisie, and second, because this collection itself reaches out to the proletarian in a most familiar and assuring manner. In it he can recognize subjects from his own history, "The Poor Governess Arrives at the House of the Wealthy Merchant," "The Police Take a Conspirator by Surprise," and the fact that these scenes are rendered entirely in the spirit of bourgeois art does not in the least detract from them — in fact it makes them far more accessible to him. The education of the eye (as Proust often makes us understand so well) is not exactly served by the contemplation of "masterworks." By contrast, the child or the proletarian who is just learning about art recognize (and rightfully so) certain things as masterpieces by criteria that are completely different from those of the collector. These paintings take on a very temporary yet solid meaning for him, and the most rigorous criterion is valid only in relation to art of the utmost relevance, which deals with him, his class, his work. — In one of the first rooms I stood for a long while in front of two paintings by Shchedrin,[112] the Sorrento harbor and another landscape of the same region; both included the indescribable silhouette of Capri, something that will always be linked in my mind to Asja. I wanted to write her a line, but I had forgotten my pencil. The immersion in subject matter that had occurred at the very outset of my visit continued to determine the spirit in which I went on to look at the other things. I saw fine portraits of Gogol, Dostoyevsky, Ostrovsky, Tolstoy. On a lower floor, which one reaches by a stairway, there were many Vereshchagin[113] to be seen. — I left the museum in a very light-hearted mood. In fact, I was already in this mood when I entered it, the primary reason for this being the brick-red church that stood near the streetcar stop. It was a cold day, but perhaps not quite as cold as the time I had first wandered over in this direction in search of the museum and had been unable to locate it, even though it was nearly staring me in the face. Finally, there was also a decent moment with Asja later that day. Reich had left shortly before seven, she had accompanied him downstairs, had remained there for a long time, and when she finally reappeared I was still there all alone, though there were only a few minutes for us to be together. I no longer remember what happened then: suddenly I was able to look at Asja with great affection and sensed how much she felt drawn to me. I gave her a brief account of what I had done all day. But I had to leave. I gave her my hand and she took it in both of hers. She would have gladly gone on talking with me, and I said to her that if I could count on her to come visit me I would cancel my plans to go see the production at Tairov's that evening. But in the end she was fairly doubtful that the doctor would let her go out. We discussed the possibility of her coming to visit me on one of the following evenings. — At Tairov's they were performing *Day and*

112. Silvestr Shchedrin (1791–1830), Russian landscape painter.
113. Vassily Vereshchagin (1842–1904), Russian painter noted for his military scenes.

Asja Lacis. (Photo courtesy Theodor W. Adorno
Archiv, Frankfurt.)

Walter Benjamin. (Photo courtesy Jewish
National and University Library, Jerusalem.)

Night after an operetta by Lecocq.[114] I met up with the American whom I had arranged to join. But I couldn't get much out of his interpreter, she was completely absorbed with him. And [since] the plot was fairly intricate, I had to content myself with the lovely ballet scenes.

January 13. The day was a washout, except for the evening. Besides, it's starting to get very cold: average temperature around [minus] twenty-six degrees Reaumur. I was freezing. Even my gloves are not much help, they are full of holes. Things were still going fairly well at the beginning of the morning. I located the travel bureau in Petrovka just as I had given up all hope, and also found out the price of tickets. Then I wanted to take the number nine bus to the toy museum. But it broke down on the Arbat and (foolishly) thinking it would be stuck there a long time, I got off. We had just passed by the Arbatskaia market, and I had been looking at it nostalgically, thinking of my first encounters with the beautiful Christmas booths of Moscow. But this time luck smiled on me here in another manner altogether. The previous evening I had gone home tired and worn out, hoping to get to my room before Reich did, only to find him there when I arrived. I was annoyed that I could not be alone even now (since our altercation about my Meyerhold article, Reich's presence often irritated me), and I immediately busied myself with moving the lamp to a chair by my bed, as I had often managed to do. The provisional [connection] to the electrical wiring again came undone; I impulsively leaned over the table and in this uncomfortable position attempted to fix the wiring, and after playing the handyman for a while I succeeded in touching off a short circuit. — There was no question of getting it repaired by the hotel. It was impossible to work by the overhead ceiling light, so the problem that had posed itself during the first days again became an issue. As I lay in bed, it dawned on me — "a candle." But even that would not be easy. It was becoming increasingly unfeasible to ask Reich to do my errands for me; he himself had a number of things to attend to, and his mood was poor. There remained the possibility of setting off on one's own, armed with a single word. But even that word would have to be first procured from Asja before proceeding. It was therefore really a stroke of luck for me to find, against all expectation, a candle on the counter of one of the booths here, and to which I had only to point. With this, however, the happy part of the day was done for. I was freezing. I wanted to go see the exhibit of graphic art at Dom Pechat:[115] closed. Ditto for the Museum of Iconography. Now I understood: it was New Year's according to the old calendar. Even as I was getting out of the sleigh that I had taken to the Museum of Iconography because it was in a remote area that I didn't know, barely able to continue any further be-

114. Alexandre Charles Lecocq (1832–1918). See note 99.
115. "Press House," a journalists' club.

cause of the cold, I realized that it was closed. In cases like this, when one's linguistic incapacitation alone pushes one to do something absurd, one becomes doubly aware of the waste of time and energy such situations involve. I discovered, closer than I had imagined, a streetcar in the opposite direction, and I made my way home. — I got to Dom Herzena before Reich. When he subsequently arrived, he greeted me with the words: "You're out of luck." He had been to the office of the *Encyclopedia* and had dropped off my piece on Goethe there. Radek[116] had happened to drop by, had seen the manuscript lying on the table, and had picked it up. Suspicious, he had inquired who had written it. "The phrase 'class conflict' occurs ten times on every page." Reich pointed out that this was not the case, and said that it was impossible to deal with Goethe's impact, which had taken place during a period of intense class conflict, without using the term. Radek: "The point is to introduce it at the right moment." In the wake of this, the chances that the piece will be accepted are extremely slim. The wretched directors of this project are far too insecure to permit themselves any possibility of a personal opinion, even when faced with the feeblest joke by someone in a position of authority. The incident was more unpleasant for Reich than for me. It only began to sink in for me when I discussed it with Asja that afternoon. She immediately started off by saying that there must have been some justification for what Radek had said. I certainly must have gone wrong somewhere, I didn't know how one had to go about things here, and other comments of the sort. Then I told her straight to her face that her words merely expressed her cowardice and her need to bend, at whatever cost, wherever the wind was blowing. Shortly after Reich arrived I left the room. I knew he was going to tell her about what had happened and I didn't want him to do so in my presence. I was hoping that Asja would come visit me that evening, so I mentioned this to her as I was leaving, despite the presence of Reich. I bought all sorts of things: caviar, cakes, sweets, even presents for Daga, whom Reich was going to drive out to see the following day. Then I settled down in my room, ate dinner, and wrote. Shortly after eight I had already given up all hope that Asja would come. It had been a long time since I had waited for her like this (in fact, given the circumstances, since I had been able to wait for her at all). And I had just started to sketch out a schematic image of my waiting for her when there was a knock at the door. It was Asja and her first words were that they had not wanted to let her in. At first I thought she was talking about my hotel. A new Sovietdushi[117] has just moved in here and seems to want to run things according to the book. But she was referring to Ivan Petrovich.[118] So that even this evening, or rather this brief hour, was hemmed in on all sides

---

116. Karl Radek (1885–1939), a leading Party official, member of the Comintern presidium in 1920, banished as a Trotskyite in 1927.
117. A term for a hotel porter.
118. Asja Lacis's doctor?

and I was fighting against time. It is true, I was victorious in the first passage of arms. I quickly sketched out the overall scheme I had in mind and as I explained it to her she pressed her forehead close against mine. Then I read her the piece I had written, and this too went quite well, she liked it, she even thought it was extraordinarily clear and concrete. I discussed the particular interest that the "Goethe" issue held for me: how a man like Goethe, whose entire life had been so caught up in compromises, had nonetheless been capable of such an extraordinary achievement. And I added that anything similar would be unthinkable for a proletarian writer. The class conflict of the bourgeoisie was, I maintained, fundamentally different from that of the proletarian, and one could not automatically equate the notions of "disloyalty" or "compromises" in these two movements. I mentioned Lukács's thesis that historical materialism was at base only applicable to the history of the workers' movement.[119] But Asja was quickly getting tired. So I resorted to the *Moscow Diary* and read her random passages that happened to catch my eye. But things went less well in this case. I had chanced upon the part where I dealt with communist education. "It's utter nonsense," said Asja. She was annoyed and claimed I knew nothing about Russia. Obviously I could not argue with this. Then she herself began to speak: what she was saying was important, but she became very agitated as she talked. She spoke of how she herself had not understood Russia in the least at the outset, how she had wanted to go back to Europe a few weeks after her arrival because everything seemed finished in Russia and the opposition was absolutely correct. Gradually she had realized what was in fact taking place here: the conversion of revolutionary effort into technological effort. Now it is made clear to every communist that at this hour revolutionary work does not signify conflict or civil war, but rather electrification, canal construction, creation of factories. I replied by bringing up Scheerbart, since I had already endured so much talk on account of him from Reich and Asja: no other author had so clearly emphasized the revolutionary character of technological achievement. (I regret not having used this excellent formulation in the interview.) With all this I managed to delay the time of her departure by a few minutes. Then she left and, as sometimes happens when she has felt close to me, she did not invite me to accompany her. I remained in the room. The two candles, which I keep lit in the evening ever since the shortcircuit, had remained on the table the whole time. Later, when I was already in bed, Reich arrived.

January 14. This day and the following one were disagreeable. The clock is set for "departure." It is getting colder and colder (the average temperature is

---

119. See Georg Lukács, *History and Class Consciousness*, translated by Rodney Livingstone, Cambridge, M.I.T. Press, 1971, which first appeared in Germany in 1923. Benjamin's brief review of the book may be found in *GS*, III, p. 171.

Wooden model of sewing machine.

under [minus] twenty degrees) and it is becoming more difficult to fulfill my remaining obligations. The preliminary symptoms of Reich's recent illness (I still don't know what he has) have become more pronounced, so he can do less and less for me. Today, all bundled up, he drove out to see Daga. I spent the morning inspecting the three railway stations: Kursk station,[120] October station, from which the trains to Leningrad leave, and Yaroslavski station, which is where the trains to Siberia leave. The restaurant in the railway station is crowded with palms and looks out onto a waiting room painted in blue. You feel as if you were at the zoo, in the antelope pavillon. I had some tea there and thought about my departure. Sitting in front of me was a beautiful red pouch of fine Crimean tobacco which I had bought in one of the booths in front of the station. Later I hunted up some new toys. There was a peddler on the Okhotny riad selling wooden toys. It occurs to me that certain merchandise turns up in the streets in batches. For example, this was the first time I had seen wooden axes for children with designs burned into them; the next day I would notice an entire basketful of them. I bought a rather silly wooden model of a sewing machine whose "needle" is activated by turning a handle, and a papier-mâché rocking puppet on a music box, a feeble imitation of a type of toy that I had seen at the museum. Unable to stand the cold any longer, I staggered into a coffee house. It seemed to be an establishment with its own particular flavor: there was cane furniture in the small room; the food emerged from the kitchen through a little sliding door in the wall, and there was a spread of *zakuski* [appetizers] on a large counter: cold cuts, pickles, fish. There was even a display case, as in French and Italian restaurants. I did not know the names of

120. Benjamin is probably thinking of the Kazan railway station.

any of the foods I would have liked to have ordered, so I warmed up with a cup of coffee. When I left, I looked around the upper commercial lanes for the store where I had noticed the clay figurines on display during my first days here. They were still there. As I went through the passageway that leads from Revolution Square to Red Square, I took closer notice of the street vendors and made an effort to observe things that had so far escaped me: the sale of women's lingerie (corsets), of neckties, shawls, hangers. — Totally exhausted, I finally got to Dom Herzena around two, though they only start serving food around two-thirty. I went home after the meal to drop off the toys. I arrived at the sanatorium around four-thirty. As I was going up the stairs, I ran into Asja, who was in the process of leaving. She was going to her seamstress's. On the way there I told her what I had heard about Daga's health from Reich (he had come home just after me). The news was encouraging. We were walking side by side when suddenly Asja asked me if I could lend her some money. The previous day I had discussed with Reich the possibility of borrowing 150 marks from him for my trip home, so I told her I had no money, still not knowing what she needed it for. She replied that I never had any money when one needed it, proceeded to make other reproaches, mentioned the room in Riga that I should have gotten for her, etc. I was quite exhausted that day and, moreover, extremely exasperated by the subject she had so tactlessly broached. It turned out that she wanted the money to rent an apartment she had heard was available. I wanted to turn off in another direction, but she held me back, hanging on to me as she had almost never done before, not letting up on the topic. Finally, beside myself with anger, I told her that she had lied to me. She had assured me by letter that she would immediately reimburse me for my expenses in Berlin, and so far neither she nor Reich had so much as breathed a word about this. This struck home. I became more violent, continued to pursue my attack, in the midst of which she finally bolted and rushed off down the street. I did not follow her; instead I took a sharp right and proceeded home. — I had an appointment with Gnedin that evening. He was going to come fetch me and take me back to his place. He was true to his word, but we ended up staying in my room. He apologized for not inviting me over to his house: his wife was preparing for an exam and had no time to spare. We talked until eleven or so, for about three hours. I began by mentioning how depressed and upset I was that I had learned so much less about Russia than I had expected. And we both agreed that the only way of getting a real picture of the situation would be to talk to a great number of people. He took it upon himself to introduce me to this and that before I left. For example, he promised to meet me at noon the next day — a Sunday — at the Proletkult Theater. But when I got there, he was nowhere to be found, so I returned home. He also promised to invite me to a performance at a club whose date, however, had not yet been fixed. The projected program involved several so to speak experimental ceremonies for the giving of names, for marriages, etc. Let me add here what Reich recently told me concerning the names of babies in the communist hierarchy. From the time they are able to point to Lenin's picture, they receive the name *oktiabre*. That evening I learned another strange term, namely the expression "have beens" [*byvshie liudi*], applied to those citizens who were dispossessed by the Revolution and who have been unable to adapt to the new situation. Gnedin furthermore spoke of the continual organizational changes that will go on taking place for years. Every week new organizational modifications are introduced and great efforts are made to come up with the best methods. We also discussed the withering away of private life. There is simply not time enough for it. Gnedin told me that the only people he sees during the week are those he deals with in the course of his work, and his wife and child. Other contacts are restricted to Sundays, but these are unstable because if you lose touch with your acquaintances even for only three weeks, you can become entirely convinced that you have not heard from them for ages because in the meantime they have supplanted old acquaintances with new ones. Later I accompanied Gnedin to the station and we spoke about customs procedures as we made our way along the street.

January 15. A futile trip to the toy museum. It was closed despite the fact that according to the guide it was open Sundays. The *Literarische Welt* finally arrived in the morning — via Hessel. I had been waiting for it so impatiently that day after day I had been considering telegraphing Berlin to send it. Asja did not understand the *Wandkalender*,[121] nor did Reich particularly seem to like it. I again spent the morning wandering around, tried for the second time to get into the graphics exhibition, and finally made it to the Shchukin Gallery,[122] half frozen. Its founder was, like his brother, a textile magnate and a multimillionaire. Both were patrons of the arts. One of them was responsible for the creation of the Historical Museum (as well as for a portion of this collection), the other one established this extraordinary gallery of modern French art. As one climbs the stairs, frozen through and through, one glimpses at the top of the stairwell the famous Matisse murals, naked figures rhythmically arranged against a background of concentrated red as warm and as luminous as that of Russian icons. Matisse, Gauguin, and Picasso were the major passions of this collector. One room has twenty-nine Gauguins crammed on its walls. (I once again came to the realization — inasmuch as this term is applicable to my rapid sampling of this great collection — that Gauguin's paintings seem hostile to me, directing all the hate against me that a non-Jew can feel toward Jews.) — There is prob-

121. Benjamin's "Wandkalender" ("Wall Calendar") appeared in the *Literarische Welt* on December 12, 1926; his verse was illustrated by Rudolph Grossmann. The same issue of the newspaper also included Benjamin's review of Lenin's *Letters to Maxim Gorky* 1908–1913.
122. Sergei Ivanovich Shchukin (1854–1936), collected fifty-four Picasso paintings between 1908–1914.

ably no other place in the world that provides one with such an overview of Picasso's development, from the early paintings of his twenties through 1914. There must have been months on end, for example during the "yellow period,"[123] when Picasso was painting solely for Shchukin. His paintings fill three contiguous rooms. In the first of these are his early works, among which there were two that struck me: a man dressed like a Pierrot, holding something like a goblet clasped in his right hand, and a painting of a female *Absinthe Drinker*. Then the cubist period around 1911 as Montparnasse was getting underway, and finally the yellow period, including, among other things, the *Amitié* and the various studies relating to it. Not far from this is an entire room devoted to Derain. Next to some very beautiful paintings in his standard manner, I saw one that was utterly disconcerting: *Le Samedi*. This large, somber canvas depicts women in Flemish costumes gathered around a table and engaged in some sort of domestic activity. Both the figures and the expression strongly recall Memling. With the exception of the small room devoted to Rousseau, all the others are extremely bright. Windows with large undivided panes look out onto the street and onto the courtyard of the building. Here for the first time I caught a rapid glimpse of such painters as Van Dongen or Le Fauconnier. The physiological configuration of a small canvas by Marie Laurencin — the head of a woman, her hand extending into the painting, a flower rising out of it — reminded me of Münchhausen[124] and made his former love of Marie Laurencin obvious to me. — At noon I learned from Nieman that my interview had appeared.[125] Thus armed with the *Vecherniaia Moskva* and the *Literarische Welt* I went to visit Asja. Still, the afternoon did not turn out well. Reich only arrived much later. Asja translated the interview for me. I had in the meantime realized — not that it might in fact appear "dangerous" as Reich had claimed, but nonetheless — that the interview's conclusion was weak, less because of the mention of Scheerbart than because of the tentative and imprecise nature of this mention. Unfortunately this weakness was immediately evident, whereas the beginning, which confronted Italian art, came off well. But on the whole I think it's a good thing that it appeared. Asja was quite taken by the beginning, but was justifiably annoyed with the end. But the main thing is that it was given a very prominent presentation. Because of our quarrel the previous day, I had purchased

123. Not the standard term, but Benjamin is obviously referring to the canvasses of Picasso's period of "synthetic cubism," roughly 1911–1914.
124. Thankmar von Munchhausen (1892-1972) "discovered" Marie Laurencin through the art historian Wilhelm Uhde. Munchhausen's correspondence with Benjamin remains unpublished. A friend of Hofmansthal and Rilke, Munchhausen arranged for Benjamin to translate St. John Perse's *Anabase*. The translation was credited to Benjamin and Bernard Groethuysen and appeared posthumously in *Das Lot*, IV (October 1950), pp. 60–74.
125. After an extensive search in libraries throughout Western Europe and North America, the editor has been unable to obtain a copy of the issue of *Vecherniaia Moskva* containing Benjamin's interview. The Lenin Library in Moscow has refused several requests for a copy of this interview.

some cake for Asja on the way over. She accepted it. Later she informed me that after we had split up yesterday she had never wanted to hear my name again and was convinced we would never see each other again (or at least not for a long while). But by the evening, to her own amazement, her mood had changed and she discovered how utterly incapable she was of being angry with me for any length of time. Whenever anything went wrong between us, she always ended up asking herself whether she had not in fact been the offender. Unfortunately, despite these words we later quarreled, I no longer remember why.

January 15 (continued).[126] In short: after I had shown Asja the newspaper and the magazine, talk of course again turned to the disappointments of my stay here, and when the conversation once more got around to my affairs in Berlin which Asja found fault with, I lost all self-control and rushed out of the room in desperation. But I came to my senses while still in the hallway — or more precisely, I didn't feel the strength to leave and returned, saying "I would just like to sit here very quietly for a bit longer." Then we even gradually managed to resume our conversation and by the time Reich arrived we were both exhausted but calm. I was determined that under no circumstances would I hereafter let myself get drawn into similar quarrels. Reich said he was not feeling well. In fact the cramp in his jaw had not let up or was getting worse. He could no longer chew. His gums were inflamed and an abscess had developed. But despite this, he said it was imperative that he go to the German club that evening because he had been appointed mediator between the German division of the VAPP and the Moscow cultural delegates of the Volga Germans. When we were alone in the lobby he told me he was also running a fever. I felt his forehead and made it clear to him that under no circumstances could he go to the club. He therefore sent me in his place to offer his apologies. The building was not far away, but the wind was so biting that I was barely able to make any headway. And in the end I was unable to find the place. I came back exhausted and stayed home.

January 16. I had fixed Friday the 21st as the date for my departure. The fact that the end of my stay was approaching made my day quite strenuous. There were many things to settle in short order. I had two things planned for Sunday. Not only would I meet Gnedin around one o'clock at the Proletkult Theater,[127] but I would also visit the Museum of Painting and Iconography (Ostrukhov)[128]

126. There is a nearly two-page blank space in the manuscript here.
127. Abbreviation of Proletarskaia Kultura, an organization devoted to promoting the "hidden creative forces" of the proletariat. Created in October 1917, it lost its political independence in 1921 when it was incorporated into the Narkompros. In 1932 it was dissolved.
128. Ilya Semyonovich Ostrukhov (1858–1929), Russian painter, curator of the Tretiakov Gallery from 1905–1913.

before that. The latter plan finally worked out, but not the former. It was again
very cold and a thick layer of ice had rendered the windows of the streetcar
opaque. I proceeded to ride far past the stop at which I should have gotten off.
And then back again. Luckily it turned out that there was a guard at the
museum who spoke German and who showed me through the collection. I only
devoted a few minutes toward the end to the ground floor, where the Russian
paintings of the end of the last century and the beginning of this one were hanging. I did well to go right upstairs to look at the icon collection, which is situated
in a lovely bright room on the second floor of this low house. The owner of the
collection is still alive. The Revolution left his museum intact; of course, it was
expropriated, [but] he was kept on as director of the collection. This Ostrukhov
is a painter and made his first acquisitions forty years ago. He was a multimillionaire, traveled all over the world, and finally decided to start collecting old
Russian wood sculpture around the time the war broke out. The oldest item in
his collection, a Byzantine portrait of a saint painted in wax colors on a wooden
board, dates back to the sixth century. The majority of the paintings date from
the fifteenth or sixteenth centuries. Under the instruction of my guide, I was
made aware of the principle differences between the Stroganov and Novogorod
schools, and a number of iconographic questions were explained to me. For the
first time I noticed the allegory of death vanquished at the foot of the cross,
which occurs so frequently in these icons. Against a background of black (as if
reflected in a murky pool), a death's head. A few days later in the icon collection of the Historical Museum I would see other depictions that were quite remarkable from an iconographic point of view. For example, a still life of the in-
struments of martyrdom, and on the altar around which these are grouped the
Holy Ghost moves in the shape of a dove on a piece of fabric painted a splendid
pink. Then, two terrifying, grotesque figures at Christ's side: clearly the thieves
that are thus designated as having entered paradise. Another depiction that frequently reoccurred — three angels at their meal with the slaughter of a lamb
inevitably in the foreground, reduced in scale and at the same time emblemat-
ically charged — remained unclear to me. The subject matter of the legendary
paintings of course eludes me completely. When I finally returned downstairs
from the rather chilly upper floor, I found that a fire had been lit in the fireplace
and the small group of employees was sitting around it, whiling away their
Sunday morning. I would have gladly stayed on, but I had to go out into the
cold. The final stretch from the telegraph office — it was there that I had gotten off — to the Proletkult Theater was awful. Then I stood watch in the
lobby for an hour. I waited in vain. A few days later I learned that Gnedin had
been waiting for me in the very same room. It is almost impossible to explain
how this could have happened. It is conceivable that exhausted as I was and
given my poor memory for faces, I didn't recognize him in his coat and cap, but
that the same thing should have occurred to him sounds implausible. I then proceeded homeward; I had initially wanted to grab a bite at our Sunday tavern,

but I missed the stop and was feeling so drained that I preferred skipping lunch to having to walk the distance on foot. But in Triumfalnaia Square I gathered up my courage and opened the door of a *stolovaia* [cafeteria] that I was not familiar with. It looked quite hospitable and the food I ordered was not bad, although the borscht clearly didn't measure up to the one we normally ate on Sundays. I had thus found the time to take a long rest before visiting Asja. When she informed me, immediately as I entered her room, that Reich was sick, I was hardly surprised. He had not stayed at my place the previous evening, but had gone instead to the room of Asja's companion at the sanatorium. Now he was bedridden and Asja soon went off to visit him with Manya. I left them at the door of the sanatorium. At which point Asja asked me what I had planned for the evening. "Nothing," I said, "I'm staying home." She made no reply. I went over to Basseches's. He was not there; he had left a note asking me to wait for him. This suited me well; I sat in the armchair with my back to the nearby stove, had myself served some tea, and leafed through the German magazines. He arrived an hour later. But then he asked me to stay the evening.

The Historical Museum.

I weighed the matter very nervously. On the one hand, since another guest was expected, I was curious what the evening would bring. In addition, Basseches was in the process of giving me some useful information about Russian film. And last but not least, I was looking forward to a dinner. (This expectation would be later dashed.) It proved impossible to inform Asja by telephone that I was at Basseches's; there was no answer at the sanatorium. Finally a messenger was dispatched: I was afraid he would get there too late and that I still would be left hanging as to whether or not Asja in fact wanted to come visit me. The following day she told me that this had indeed been her intention. But at any rate, she got the note in time. It read: "Dear Asja, I am spending the evening at Basseches's. I will be by tomorrow at four o'clock. Walter." I had originally written "evening" and "at" [*abends bei*] as a single word, and then had placed a diagonal dividing line between the two. With the result that Asja initially read it as "I am free this evening" [*abends frei*]. — Later a certain Dr. Kroneker showed up; he works here as the Austrian representative of a large Russo-Austrian firm. Basseches told me he was a Social Democrat. But he struck me as quite intelligent, had traveled widely, and spoke to the point. In the course of the conversation, we got on to the subject of gas warfare. I made a number of comments that impressed them both.

January 17. The most important outcome of my visit to Basseches the previous day was that I managed to convince him to help me with the formalities of my departure. He had, as a result, asked me to drop by early on Monday (the 16th). I arrived and he was still in bed. It was very difficult to rouse him. And it was a quarter to one before we finally got to Triumfalnaia Square; I had showed up at his place as early as eleven. Prior to that I had had some coffee and cake in my regular pastry shop. This was a good thing because with all the errands, I would miss lunch that day. We first went to a bank on Petrovka because Basseches needed to withdraw some money. I changed money myself, keeping only fifty marks in reserve. Then Basseches took me along to a small office in order to introduce me to a bank director he knew, a certain Dr. Schick,[129] director of the foreign division. This man had lived in Germany for a very long time, had studied there, no doubt comes from a very wealthy background, and, above and beyond his specialized training, had always maintained an interest in the arts. He had read my interview in the *Vecherniaia Moskva*. As chance would have it, he had known Scheerbart personally during his German student days. Contact was thus immediately established and our brief discussion ended with an invitation to dinner on the 20th. Then to Petrovka, where I obtained

---

129. Maximilien Schick (1884–1968), poet and translator into German of Briusov, Gorky, and others. He lived in Germany from 1892–1907, and contributed to the Russian symbolist magazine *Vesy* (*Scales*).

my passport. After that, by sleigh to Narkompros,[130] where I got my papers validated for the border crossing. It was on this day that I finally succeeded in an important project: I was able to persuade Basseches to take another sleigh and accompany me to the upper shopping levels of the state store "GUM," where the dolls and riders I had been eyeing were located. Together we bought whatever was still in stock, and I picked out the ten best items for myself. Each one cost a mere ten kopeks. My keen observation had not betrayed me: they told us in the store that these articles, which are made in Viatka,[131] no longer find their way into Moscow: there is no longer a market for them here. What we bought were therefore the last of these items to be had. Basseches also purchased some peasant fabric. He went off with his packages to lunch at the Savoy, whereas I only had the time to drop everything off at home. Then it was four o'clock, time to go visit Asja. We only stayed in her room briefly before going to see Reich. Manya[132] was already with him. But at least this way we were able to have a few minutes to ourselves once again. I asked Asja to come to my place that evening — I would be free until ten-thirty — and she promised to do so if possible. Reich was feeling much better. What it was we talked about during the visit, I no longer remember. We left at about seven. After dinner I waited in vain for Asja and at about a quarter to eleven I went over to Basseches's. But there was no one there. They said he had not been back all day. All the magazines there I had either already read or found nauseating. After half an hour's wait I was just about to go downstairs when I encountered his friend, and — I do not exactly know why: perhaps because she didn't want to go to the club alone with him — she insisted that I wait a bit longer. Which I did. Then Basseches finally turned up; he had had to attend the speech that Rykov[133] had given to the Aviachim congress.[134] I had him fill out my questionnaire requesting an exit visa and then we left. On our way over I was introduced in the streetcar to a playwright, a writer of comedies, who was also going to the club. We had just found a table in the overcrowded room and the three of us were just sitting down when the lights went out, signifying that the concert was about to begin. We had to get up. I moved to the lobby with Basseches. A few minutes later — dressed in a dinner jacket, having come directly from a banquet that a large British firm had just given in the Bolshaia Moskovskaia — the German consul general appeared. He had come [to join] two women whom he had met there and with whom he had arranged a rendezvous here, but since

130. Narodnyi Komissariat Prozveshcheniia (People's Committee on Public Education).
131. Now Kirov.
132. Lacis's roommate.
133. Alexei Rykov (1881–1938) succeeded Lenin from 1924–1930 as president of the Council of the People's Commissars of the Soviet Union.
134. Abbreviation for the Obshchestvo sodeistva aviatsionno-khimicheskomu stroitelstvu v SSR (Society for the Encouragement of the Creation of the Aeronautical and Chemical Industry in the USSR).

they had not arrived, he remained with us. A woman — apparently a former princess — was singing folk songs in a beautiful voice. At one point I stood in the dark dining room by the entrance to the illuminated concert hall, at another I sat in the lobby. I exchanged a few words with the consul general, who behaved most courteously. But his face was coarse, only superficially etched with intelligence, and he perfectly fit the image of German foreign service personnel that had fixed itself in my mind ever since my ocean voyage[135] and the twin figures of Frank and Zorn. There were only four of us for dinner, and since the secretary of the embassy had joined us, I could therefore observe him at my ease. The food was good, there was again spiced vodka, as well as appetizers, two entrees, and ice cream. The crowd couldn't have been worse. A few artists — of whatever stripe — and even more members of the NEP bourgeoisie. It is striking to what extent this new bourgeoisie is held in contempt, even by foreign diplomats — at least to judge by the comments of the consul general, which seemed to me to be sincerely intended in this case. The total spiritual impoverishment of this class was evident in the dancing that followed and which was on the order of an unsavory small town shindig. The dancing was awful. Unfortunately, given Basseches's friend's impulse to dance, the fun went on until four o'clock. I was dead tired from the vodka, the coffee had not perked me up, and I had a stomach ache to top it off. I was glad when I finally found myself in a sleigh on the way back to the hotel; it was about four-thirty when I got to bed.

January 18. I visited Reich in Manya's room in the morning. There were a few things that I had to bring him. But at the same time I was coming to see him in order to allay the frictions that had occurred during the days just prior to his illness. I won him over by listening attentively to his outline for a book on politics and theater that he wants to bring out with a Russian publishing firm.[136] We also discussed plans for a book about theater architecture, a book he could have written with Poelzig[137] and which, given the amount of solid theatrical research into set design and costuming, would now be of considerable interest. Before I left I brought him up some cigarettes from the street and agreed to take care of an errand for him at Dom Herzena. Then I went to the Historical Museum. I spent over an hour here in the extraordinarily rich icon collection, where I also discovered a considerable number of later works of the seventeenth and eighteenth centuries. But how long it takes the Christ child to acquire the freedom of movement in the arms of his mother that he exercises during these later

135. Probably a reference to Benjamin's 1925 journey by steamship from Hamburg to Italy via Barcelona.
136. Reich never published this book.
137. Hans Poelzig (1869–1936), influential architect and professor at the Technische Hochschule of Charlottenberg. Among other theater constructions, Poelzig in 1919 oversaw the transformation of the Schumann circus into Max Reinhardt's Grosses Schauspielhaus in Berlin.

periods! Similarly, it takes centuries before the hand of the child finally finds the hand of the mother of God: the painters of Byzantium simply show the hands facing each other. I subsequently made a rapid tour of the archaeological section, lingering only in front of a few paintings of Mount Athos. Upon leaving the museum, I came a bit closer to grasping the mystery of the powerful effect produced by Blagoveshchenski Cathedral, which had been my first and only noteworthy impression of Moscow. Its effect derives from the fact that Red Square, when approached from the direction of Revolution Square, slopes up slightly, so that the domes of the cathedral emerge bit by bit as if from behind a mountain. It was a beautiful sunny day and it was with considerable joy that I again caught sight of the cathedral. I was unable to obtain any money for Reich at Dom Herzena. When I arrived at Asja's door at a quarter past four, everything was dark inside. I twice knocked gently and since there was no answer, I went to the recreation room to wait. I read the *Nouvelles littéraires*. When, a quarter of an hour later, there was still no answer, I opened the door and discovered there was no one there. Annoyed that Asja had already left so soon without waiting for me, I went over to Reich's in order nonetheless to make an attempt to arrange something with her for the evening. Reich had made it impossible for me to go to the Maly Theater with her as I had wanted because he had objected to my plan that morning. (Later, when I actually obtained tickets for the evening, I was unable to make any use of them.) When I got upstairs, I didn't even bother to take off my things and remained very quiet. Manya was again vehemently explaining something or other in a terribly loud voice. She was showing Reich a statistical atlas. Suddenly Asja turned and said to me point–blank that she had not come to see me yesterday evening because she was having severe headaches. I lay on the sofa in my overcoat, smoking the small pipe that I exclusively use in Moscow. I finally managed somehow to convey to Asja that she should come to my place after dinner and we would go somewhere or I would read her the lesbian scene.[138] And then I stayed on for another few minutes so it would not seem as if I had come over for the sole purpose of telling her this. I soon got up, saying I had to go. "Where?" "Home." "I thought you were going to come back to the sanatorium with us." "Aren't you staying here till seven?" I asked somewhat hypocritically, having of course heard that morning that Reich's secretary was due to arrive. I ended up staying but did not go back to the sanatorium with Asja. I thought she would be more likely to come over that evening if I gave her some time now to rest. In the meantime, I bought her caviar, tangerines, candy, and cakes. On the windowsill on which I keep my toys I had also set up two clay dolls, one of which she was to choose for herself. And in fact she did appear — initially claiming "I can only stay five minutes, I have to be back right away." But this time she was

138. The scene involving Mademoiselle de Vinteuil and her female lover in *Du côté de chez Swann*.

only teasing. To be sure, I had sensed that during the past few days — right in the wake of our violent quarrels — she had been feeling more strongly drawn to me. But I didn't know to what degree. I was in good spirits when she arrived because I had just received a lot of mail with good news from Wiegand, Müller-Lehning, and Else Heinle.[139] The letters were still on the bed where I had been reading them. Besides, Dora[140] had written that money was on its way, so I had decided to extend my stay a bit. I mentioned this to her, and she threw her arms around me. The constellation of circumstances had been so difficult for weeks that I was miles away from expecting such a gesture, and it took some time before it made me happy. I was like a vase with a slender neck into which liquid was being poured from a pail. Little by little I had so deliberately closed myself off that I was almost no longer receptive to the full power of external impressions. But this went away over the course of the evening. First I asked Asja for a kiss amid the usual protestations. But then it was as if an electrical switch had suddenly been flipped, and now as I was trying to talk or read aloud to her she kept on insisting on yet another kiss. Tendernesses that had nearly been forgotten resurfaced. Meanwhile I presented her with the food I had purchased and with the dolls; she chose one of them and it is now sitting across from her bed in the sanatorium. I also brought up the subject of my Moscow stay once again. And since she had actually uttered the decisive words the previous day as we were on our way to Reich's, I needed only to repeat them: "The place Moscow now occupies in my life is such that I can only experience it through you — this is true, regardless of any love affair, romantic interest, etc." But then again, and this she had also told me at the outset, six weeks is hardly time enough to start feeling at home in a city, especially if you don't know the language and encounter obstacles at every turn as a result. Asja had me remove the letters and she lay down on the bed. We kissed at length. But the thing that excited me the most deeply was the touch of her hands; she herself had in fact once told me that everybody who was attached to her felt the extremely powerful forces that emanated from her hands. I placed my right palm directly against her left one and we remained in this position for a long time. Asja recalled the beautiful tiny letter that I had presented to her one night in the via Depretis in Naples as we were sitting at a table in a small cafe on a nearly deserted street. I must try to locate it in Berlin. Then I read her the lesbian scene from Proust. Asja grasped its savage nihilism: how Proust in a certain fashion ventures into

---

139. Willy Wiegand (1884-1961) was cofounder of the Bremer Presse, which published the *Neue Deutsche Beitrage* in which Benjamin's essay on Goethe's *Elective Affinities* appeared in 1924–1925. Arthur Müller-Lehning (born 1899) published the journal *i 10, Internationale Revue* (Amsterdam), in which appeared an early version of Benjamin's *Einbahnstrasse* as well as his essay "New Poetry in Russia." Else Heinle, wife of Wolf Heinle (1899-1923). Benjamin was an ardent admirer of the poetry of Wolf Heinle and that of his brother Friedrich Heinle (1892-1914), and intended to publish an edition of their works.
140. Dora Sophie Benjamin (1890-1964), Benjamin's wife from 1917–1930.

the tidy private chamber within the petit bourgeois that bears the inscription *sadism* and then mercilessly smashes everything to pieces, so that nothing remains of the untarnished, clear-cut conception of wickedness, but instead within every fracture evil explicitly shows its true substance — "humanity," or even "kindness." And as I was explaining this to Asja, it became clear to me how closely this coincided with the thrust of my baroque book. Just as the previous evening, while reading alone in my room and coming across the extraordinary passage on Giotto's *Caritas*,[141] it had become clear to me that Proust was here developing a conception that corresponds at every point to what I myself have tried to subsume under the concept of allegory.

January 19. There is almost nothing to report about the day. Since my departure had been postponed, I was able to rest up a bit from the various errands and visits of the past few days. For the first time Reich again slept at my place. Asja came by in the morning but she soon had to leave for an appointment that concerned her job. During the short time she was present a discussion about gas warfare developed. At first she violently disagreed with me; but Reich intervened. In the end she said I should put my points down in writing and I promised myself to compose an article on the subject for the *Weltbühne*.[142] I left shortly after Asja. I met with Gnedin. Our conversation was brief; we discussed our mix-up on Sunday, he invited me to Vakhtangov's[143] for the following Sunday evening, and gave me a few more pointers about clearing my baggage through customs. On the way over and back from Gnedin's I passed by the Cheka[144] building. It is always patrolled by a soldier with a fixed bayonet. And then to the post office where I cabled for money. I had my midday meal in our Sunday tavern, then went home and rested. In the lobby of the sanatorium, I ran into Asja on one side and then immediately into Reich on the other. Asja had to take a bath. Reich and I played dominos in her room. Then Asja returned and told us about the perspectives that the morning had opened for her, about the possibility of her getting a job as an assistant director in a theater on Tverskaia which puts on two shows a week for proletarian children. Reich spent the evening with Illés. I did not go along. He made his appearance in my room around

141.   See *Du côté du chez Swann*, Paris, Gallimard (Pléiade), 1954, volume I, pp. 80–82.
142.   The article was never written, but see Benjamin's 1925 essay "Die Waffen von Morgen" ("The Weaponry of Tomorrow"), *GS*, IV, pp. 473–476. Kurt Tucholsky and Carl von Ossietzky became the editors of the *Weltbühne* in 1926 and turned it leftward; the Nazis shut it down in 1933. Ossietzky died in a concentration camp and Tucholsky committed suicide in Sweden in 1934.
143.   Evgeny Vakhtangov (1883–1922). The theater that bears his name was created from the third studio of the MAKHT (founded in 1921). For a period Vakhtangov also directed the Habimah (Hebrew Theater).
144.   Chrezvychainaia komissia, the state secret police.

eleven; but it was too late by then to go see a film as we had planned. Brief, somewhat fruitless conversation about the corpse in pre-Shakespearian theater.

January 20. I spent most of the morning writing in my room. [Since Reich] had to take care of a few things at the *Encyclopedia* at one o'clock, I wanted to take advantage of the occasion, not so much to lobby for my Goethe piece (I had given up all hope as far as it was concerned) as to follow up on a suggestion of Reich's and in order not to appear lazy in his eyes. Otherwise he might have also ascribed the responsibility for the rejection of my Goethe article to my lack of zeal. I could barely contain my laughter when I finally found myself sitting face to face with the professor in question. Upon learning my name he immediately sprang up, went to fetch my piece as well as a secretary to reinforce him. He began by offering me articles on the baroque. I made the acceptance of the "Goethe" entry a precondition for any further collaboration. Then I enumerated my published writings, emphasized my qualifications as Reich had advised, and just as I was in the process of doing this, Reich walked in. But he took a seat far away from me and started talking with another functionary. They would let me know of their decision in a few days. I then had to spend a long time waiting for Reich in the vestibule. Finally we left; he explained that they were planning to offer the "Goethe" entry to Walzel.[145] We went to see Pansky. It is hard to believe — but entirely possible — that he is twenty-seven years old, as Reich later informed me. The generation that was active during the period of the Revolution is growing old. It is as if the stabilization of the situation of the state had introduced into their lives a tranquility or an equanimity such as one normally only achieves in old age. Pansky, at any rate, is utterly without charm, which is apparently the case with Moscovites. My expectations were raised when he mentioned that the following Monday there would be a screening of several films that I wanted to see before writing the article against Schmitz requested by the *Literarische Welt.*[146] We went to eat. I returned home after the meal because Reich wanted to speak to Asja in private. Later I went up to visit for an hour and then proceeded on to Basseches's. The major disappointment of the evening at the home of the bank director Maximilien Schick proved to be the absence of dinner. I had eaten almost nothing for lunch and was starving. So when tea was finally served, I unabashedly stuffed myself with cake. Schick comes from a very rich family, studied in Munich, Berlin, and Paris, and served in the Russian guard. Now he lives with his wife and child in a room that has been divided into three by partitions. He is probably a fitting example of what they here call a "has been." Not only is he this from the sociological point of

145. See note 82.
146. See note 163.

Tverskaia Street with triumphal arch in background.

view (and even here he is somewhat of an exception because of his important position), but even his productive period "has been." He used to publish poems in *Die Zukunft*,[147] for example, as well as articles in magazines that are now long forgotten. But he continues to hold fast to his early passions, and his study contains a modest but well-selected library of French and German works of the nineteenth century. He mentioned what he had paid for some of the more valuable volumes and the prices indicated that the booksellers considered them junk. Over tea I tried to get some information about contemporary Russian literature out of him. My efforts were in vain. Beyond Briusov,[148] there is little that he appreciates. A small, very pretty woman who was visibly not someone who worked, sat with us. But she was not interested in books and luckily Basseches was more or less keeping her company. In return for several favors that he hopes to obtain from me in Germany, he loaded me up with worthless, uninteresting children's books, none of which I could refuse. There was only one that I accepted gladly, not that it was of any value, but it was pretty. Upon leaving, Basseches fortunately enticed me as far as Tverskaia, promising to show me a cafe frequented by prostitutes. I saw nothing of note in the cafe, but at least managed to get some cold fish and a crab to eat. I accompanied him in a luxury sleigh to the intersection of Sadovaia and Tverskaia.

147. Berlin political journal founded in 1892 by Maximilien Harden. Among its contributors were Fontane, Holz, Nietzsche, Mann, Rilke, and Hofmannsthal.
148. Valerii Briusov (1873–1924), Russian novelist.

Tverskaia Street.

January 21. This is the anniversary of Lenin's death. All the entertainment spots stay closed but because of the "economic regime" the store and office holiday falls on the following day, a Saturday, which is only half a workday anyway. I set out early to see Schick at the bank and learned that it had been arranged that I would visit Muskin[149] on Saturday to look at his collection of children's books. Changed money and went to the toy museum. This time I finally made some progress. They promised me that they would let me know on Tuesday about the photographs I wanted to have made up. But then I was shown some photos for which there were negatives available. Since they are far less expensive, I ordered about twenty of them. This time I also devoted particular attention to the clay articles from Viatka. — The previous evening, just as I was in the process of leaving, Asja had invited me to join her at the children's theater that puts on performances in the Ars cinema building on Tverskaia. But when I got there, the theater was deserted; I realized that it was unlikely that there would be a show today. Informing me that the theater was closed, a guard finally kicked me out of the lobby, where I had been trying to warm up. After I had been waiting outside for some time, Manya turned up with a note from Asja, which said that she had made a mistake and that the performance was Saturday and not Friday. With Manya's help, I proceeded to buy some candles. My eyes were already thoroughly inflamed by the candlelight. Wanting to gain

149. Director of the children's books division of the State Publishing House.

Ars cinema on Tverskaia Street.

some time for work, I did not go to Dom Herzena (which at any rate was probably closed today), but instead lunched in the neighborhood *stolovaia*. The meal was expensive but not bad. When I got back to my room I did not work on the Proust as I had intended,[150] but rather on a reply to the ugly, insolent obituary that Franz Blei had composed on Rilke.[151] Later I read what I had written to Asja and her comments encouraged me to rework it that very evening and the following day. She was, by the way, not feeling well. — Later I took Reich to the same restaurant at which I had had lunch. It was the first time he had eaten there. Then we went shopping. He spent the evening with me at my place until about eleven-thirty, and we got into a conversation during which each of us in turn went into detail about what we remembered of our boyhood readings. He was sitting in the armchair, I was lying on the bed. In the course of this conversation it dawned on me that for some curious reason, even as a boy I was already reading things that were not the ordinary fare. Hoffmann's

150. This most likely refers to Benjamin's ongoing Proust translation rather than to the essay on Proust which he had long been contemplating. He writes in a letter of September 18, 1926: "I don't know how long I've had the idea in mind to write an essay 'On Translating Marcel Proust' and just recently in Marseilles the *Cahiers du Sud* agreed to take it. Basically it will deal less with translation than with Proust." The essay was completed only in 1929. See "The Image of Proust" in *Illuminations*, edited and with an introduction by Hannah Arendt, New York, Harcourt, Brace, and World, 1968.
151. Benjamin's reply to Blei was not published during his lifetime. It may be found in *GS*, IV, pp. 453–454; Blei's "Zu Rainer Maria Rilke" can be found on pp. 1025–1027.

Neuer deutscher Jugendfreund[152] is practically the only standard children's book of the period that I read. And of course also the excellent Hoffmann series, *Lederstrumpf*,[153] Schwab's *Sagen des klassischen Altertums*.[154] But I did not read more than one book by Karl May,[155] nor am I familiar with the *Kampf um Rom* or the sea stories of Wörishöffer.[156] And I only read one book by Gerstäcker,[157] which must have contained a rather steamy love story (or did I only read it because I had heard this about one of the author's other books?), to be exact, *Die Regulatoren von Arkansas*. I also discovered that my entire knowledge of classical theater goes back to my reading circle days.[158]

January 22. I had not yet washed but was sitting at my table writing when Reich arrived. It was a morning on which I was even less inclined to be sociable than usual. I barely allowed myself to be distracted from my work. But when I was about to leave around twelve-thirty and Reich asked me where I was off to, I discovered that he too was going to the children's theater to which Asja had invited me. The sum total of my preferential treatment thus turned out to be a futile half hour wait at the entrance that previous day. Nonetheless I went on ahead to get something warm to drink in my usual cafe. But the cafes were also closed that day, and this, too, is part of the *remont* policy. So I slowly made my way down Tverskaia to the theater. Reich arrived later, and then Asja with Manya. Since we had now become a foursome, I lost interest in the thing. I couldn't stay to the end anyway because I had to meet Schick at three-thirty. Nor did I make any effort to take a seat beside Asja; instead I sat between Reich and Manya. Asja asked Reich to translate the dialogue for me. The play seemed to be about the creation of a cannery and appeared to have a strong chauvinistic bias against England. I left during the intermission. At which point Asja even offered me the seat next to hers as an inducement to stay, but I didn't want to arrive late or, even more important, turn up exhausted for my appointment with Schick. He himself was not quite ready. In the bus he spoke of his Paris days, how Gide had once visited him, etc. The visit with Muskin

---

152. Franz Hoffmann (1814–1882), *Neuer deutscher Jugendfreund zur Unterhaltung und Belehrung der Jugend*, a mid-nineteenth-century children's classic.
153. German title of James Fenimore Cooper's *Leather-Stocking Tales*.
154. Gustav Schwab, *Die schönsten Sagen des klassischen Altertums* (1838), a German Bulfinch.
155. Karl May (1842–1912), author of immensely popular adventure stories set in the American West.
156. Felix Dahn's *Kampf um Rom*. Sophie Wörishöffer (1838–1890), author of maritime adventure novels.
157. Friedrich Gerstäcker (1816–1872), author of exotic adventure stories.
158. According to Gershom Scholem, from 1908–1914 Benjamin and his circle of friends — Herbert Belmore, Alfred Steinfeld, Franz Sachs, and Willi Wolfradt — conducted a weekly evening of reading in which works by Shakespeare, Hebbel, Strindberg, Ibsen, and Wedekind were read and discussed.

was well worth it. Although I only saw one truly important children's book, a Swiss children's calendar of 1837, a thin little volume with three very beautiful color plates, I nevertheless looked through so many Russian children's books that I was able to get an idea of what their illustrations were like. The great majority of them are copies of German models. The illustrations in many of the books were printed by German lithography shops. Many German books were imitated. The Russian editions of *Struwwelpeter*[159] that I saw there were quite coarse and ugly. Muskin placed slips of paper in various books on which he noted down my comments. He directs the children's book division of the state publishing house. He showed me some samples of his work. They included books for which he himself had written the text. I explained to him the broad outlines of my documentary project on "Fantasy."[160] He didn't seem to understand much of what I was saying and on the whole made a rather mediocre impression on me. His library was in lamentable shape. There was not enough room to set up the books properly, so they were strewn every which way on shelves in the hallway. There was a fairly rich assortment of food on the tea table and without any prodding I ate a great deal, since I had eaten neither lunch nor dinner that day. We stayed for about two and a half hours. Before I left he presented me with two books he had published and which I silently promised to give to Daga. Spent the evening back home working on the Rilke and the diary. But — as is the case at this very moment — with such poor writing materials that nothing comes to mind.

January 23. (It's been some time since I've kept this diary, so I have to summarize things.) This was the day that Asja made the various arrangements for leaving the sanatorium. She was moving in with Rachlin; and thus had at last found an agreeable environment. Over the course of the following days I was able to measure the possibilities Moscow might have offered me had the doors of a house such as this been open to me earlier. Now it was too late to take any advantage of them. Rachlin lives in a very clean, spacious room in the building that houses the Central Archives. She lives with a student who is said to be very poor and does not want to live with her out of pride. Wednesday, only two days after we had first met, she gave me a Caucasian dagger as a gift, a very beautiful piece of silver work, even though it was intended for children and not of great value. Asja claimed that she was to thank for this present. At any rate, Asja was no more accessible to me during the period she stayed with Rachlin than she had been at the sanatorium. There was an ever-present Red Army gen-

159. A classic mid-nineteenth-century children's book by Heinrich Hoffmann (1809–1894); translated into English as *Slovenly Peter* by Mark Twain, Edward Lear, and others.
160. Benjamin apparently never carried out this project, although the theme of childhood fantasy is crucial to his *Berliner Chronik* (1932).

Streetcar stop on Strasnoi Square.

eral who had only been married two months but who was courting Asja in every conceivable fashion and who had asked her to run off with him to Vladivostok, where he was being transferred. He said he wanted to leave his wife behind in Moscow. On one of these days, Monday to be exact, Asja received a letter from Astachov that had been sent from Tokyo and forwarded from Riga by Elvira. On Thursday, as we were both leaving Reich, she told me its contents in detail, and she again brought the letter up that evening. She is apparently very much on Astachov's mind and since she had asked him to get her a shawl with cherry blossoms on it, he had probably — or so I said — spent half a year looking at nothing but cherry blossom shawls in Tokyo shopwindows. That morning I dictated the note attacking Blei as well as several letters. I was in a very good mood that afternoon, talked to Asja, but only remember that just after I had left her room in order to take her suitcase back to my place, she followed me out the door and gave me her hand. I have no idea what she was expecting from me, perhaps nothing at all. It was only the following day that I realized that Reich had cooked up an entire scheme so that I would be the one to transport the suitcase because he was feeling ill. Two days later, after Asja's move, he took to bed in Manya's room. But he is rapidly recovering from his flu. I therefore had to go on depending entirely on Basseches for the various arrangements concerning my departure. A quarter of an hour after I left the sanatorium we met at the bus station. I had made plans to go to the Vakhtangov Theater that evening with Gnedin, but had to accompany Reich along to his secretary because I wanted to make use of her services the following morning during the screenings at the Gos cinema. Everything worked out. Then Reich put me in a sleigh and I went to the Vakhtangov. Gnedin and his wife arrived a quarter of an hour after the performance had begun. I was just about to make up my mind to leave and, remembering the previous Sunday at the Proletkult Theater, I had begun wondering whether Gnedin was crazy. But now there were no more tickets to be had. Finally he managed to come up with a few; but we didn't sit together and over the course of the various acts, we engaged in every possible permutation of seating, since there were two adjacent spots and another one off on its own. Gnedin's wife was plump, friendly, and reserved, and despite her extremely plain features, not without charm. After the performance they both accompanied me to Smolensk Ploshchad, where I took a streetcar.

January 24. It was an exhausting, unpleasant day in every respect, even though I was in the end able to accomplish almost all of my objectives. The day began with my having to wait around interminably at the Gos cinema. Two hours later the screening began. I saw *Mother, Potemkin,* and part of *The Trial of the Three Million.*[161] The whole thing cost me a *chervonets*: out of consideration for Reich, I wanted to give something to the translator he had arranged for me, but she named no sum even though I had kept her on for five hours. It was quite a chore sitting through that many films in succession with no musical accompaniment and in a small screening room where we constituted virtually the entire audience. I met Reich in Dom Herzena. He went to visit Asja after lunch, I waited for them at home and then we were all going to go over to Rachlin's together. But only Reich showed up, so I went out to pick up the money that had been cabled to the local post office. This took about an hour. The scene would be worth describing. The employee was dealing with my money order as if I were trying to rob her of her favorite child, and had not a woman who spoke some French intervened at the counter after a while, I would have left empty-handed. I returned to the hotel exhausted. A few minutes later we set off for Rachlin's, loaded down with suitcases, coats, and blankets. Asja had in the meantime gone there directly. There was a considerable gathering present: in addition to the Red general, there was a friend of Rachlin's who wanted me to deliver something to a Parisian friend of hers, a painter. The strain did not abate, for Rachlin — who is not a disagreeable person — kept on talking at me; and meanwhile, dimly aware of how much interest the general was showing in Asja, I was continuously trying to keep a watch on what was going on between them. And in addition to all this, there was the presence of Reich. I had to give up all hope of having a word in private with Asja; the few words I did exchange with her as I was leaving were meaningless. I subsequently stopped by at Basseches's for a moment to discuss some technical matters concerning my departure, and then went home. Reich slept in Manya's room.

---

161. *Mother*, a 1926 film adaptation by Vsevolod I. Pudovkin of Gorky's 1906 novel. *The Trial of the Three Million*, a 1926 detective comedy directed by Yakov Protazanov.

January 25. The scarcity of living quarters here creates a strange effect: unlike in other cities, here the streets in the evening are lined with large and small houses with almost every window lit up. If the glow cast by these windows were not so uneven, you might imagine you were looking at an illumination. There is another thing I've noticed these past few days: it is not merely the snow that might possibly make you nostalgic for Moscow, but also the sky. In no other metropolis do you have so much sky overhead. The low buildings largely contribute to this. In this city you always sense the vast horizon of the Russian steppes. Something new and delightful: a boy on the street carrying a board with stuffed birds. So they also sell these sorts of birds on the streets. Even more curious was the "red" funeral procession I came across on the street that day. The coffin, the hearse, the horse's bridles were all red. On another occasion I saw a streetcar painted with political propaganda images, unfortunately it went by so quickly that I was unable to make out the details. The degree to which the exotic surges forth from the city is always astounding. I see as many Mongol faces as I wish every day in my hotel. But recently there were figures standing out in front of it on the street, garbed in red and yellow coats, Buddhist priests, Basseches informed me, in Moscow for the moment to attend a congress. The ticket collectors in the streetcars, on the other hand, remind me of the primitive peoples of the North. They stand at their spot in the car, enveloped in furs like Samoyed women on their sleds. — I managed to take care of various matters that day. The morning was devoted to preparations for my departure. I had stupidly gotten my passport photos stamped, so I now had my picture taken at a rush photographer's on Strasnoi Boulevard. Then various other errands. The previous evening at Rachlin's I had gotten in touch with Illés and arranged to meet him at Narkompros. After some effort, I located him. We lost a great deal of time going on foot from the ministry to Gosfilm, where Illés had to speak with Pansky. I had just hit upon the unhappy idea of acquiring stills from *One-Sixth of the World* from Gosfilm and I conveyed this request to Pansky. Whereupon he began feeding me the most abstruse line: the film was not to be mentioned abroad, its footage contained clips from foreign films, their precise provenance was not even clear, and complications were to be feared — in short, he was making an enormous issue out of it. He then proceeded to urge Illés in the strongest possible fashion to work together with him immediately in getting the filming of *Attentat* underway. But Illés courteously stuck to his rejection of the proposal, and so I was finally able to get a chance to talk with him at a nearby cafe (Lux). The conversation proved as productive as I had hoped: he provided me with a very interesting outline of contemporary literary groups in Russia, based on the political orientations of the various authors. Then I immediately went to see Reich. I again spent the evening at Rachlin's place, Asja had asked me to come by. I was utterly exhausted and took a sleigh. When I got upstairs, there was the unavoidable Ilyusha,[162] who had gone out and pur-

162. I.e., the general.

Strasnoi Square.

chased a mountain of sweets. I had not brought any vodka along as Asja had
asked me to; port wine was all I had been able to find. That day as well as the
following ones we had long telephone conversations which recalled the ones we
used to have in Berlin. Asja absolutely loves to say important things by telephone. She spoke of wanting to live with me in the Grunewald and was very
upset when I told her it wouldn't work out. This was the evening Rachlin gave
me the Caucasian dagger. I stayed on until Ilyusha left: I was not in the best of
spirits; they later rose somewhat when Asja came to sit by me on a love seat,
the kind you sit in back to back to the person beside you. But she was kneeling
on her seat and had wrapped my silk Parisian scarf around her. I had unfortunately already eaten dinner at home, so I could not partake of many of the delicacies arrayed on the table.

January 26. A stretch of days with wonderful warm weather. Moscow is again drawing much nearer to me. I feel the desire to learn Russian, just as I did during the first days of my stay. It is very warm but the sun is not blinding, so it is easier for me to observe what is going on around me on the streets and I consider each day a gift that has been given to me two or three times over because each is so beautiful, because Asja is now often near to me, and because each is a day I have granted myself beyond the planned duration of my stay. So I am therefore seeing many new things. Above all, more peddlers: a man with a bundle of children's pistols hanging from his shoulders, shooting off one of them from time to time, the shot echoing down the street through the clear air. Also many peddlers selling baskets of all sorts, colored baskets that look somewhat like the ones you can buy everywhere in Capri, double-handled baskets of strict geometrical design, four colorful motifs framed within their squares. I also saw a man with a large suitcase whose wicker was interwoven with strands of green and red straw; but he was not a peddler. — This morning I tried without success to expedite my trunk at the custom's office. Since I didn't have my passport with me (it had been consigned to obtain my exit visa), they agreed only to take the trunk but not to clear it. I was unable to get anything settled all morning, had lunch in the small cellar restaurant, and went to see Reich in the afternoon and brought him along some apples at Asja's request. I didn't see Asja all day but I had two long telephone conversations with her in the afternoon and evening. Spent the evening working on my rejoinder to Schmitz's essay on *Potemkin*.[163]

January 27. I am still wearing Basseches's coat. — This was an important day. I went to the toy museum again that morning and chances are now good that something can be worked out with the photographs. I saw the objects that

163. Published as "Eine Diskussion über russische Filmkunst und kollektivistische Kunst überhaupt" in the *Literarische Welt*, March 11, 1927 (see *GS*, II, pp. 751–755). A rough draft of this article was made on the final page of the *Moscow Diary* manuscript. After drawing a sarcastic portrait of Schmitz as a petit-bourgeois intellectual, Benjamin goes on to refute his criticisms of *Potemkin*: "Objectively, one could discuss *Potemkin* just as well from the political as from the cinematic point of view. But Schmitz does neither. He only talks about what he has been reading recently. But the social novels of Wassermann (or anybody else) have about as much to do with the social content of *Potemkin* as does Stower's (or anybody else's) navy with the maneuvers of this battleship in the Black Sea. Such a comparison proves nothing. The objection against *Tendenz-kunst* [politically partisan art] is far more evident. For to put it in plain German: isn't it about time to get rid of this bourgeois bogeyman once and for all? Why bemoan the political deflowering of art now that we have tracked down two thousand years of creative sublimations, Oedipus complexes, libidinal leftovers, and infantile regressions? But this is how the bourgeois theory runs in a period of decadence: art can venture as much as it likes into the most disreputable back alleys as long as it remains a good girl in politics and does not start dreaming of class warfare. But to no avail: art is always dreaming of this. The only important thing is that, what with the awakening of new regions of consciousness, this so-called 'partisan tendency' [*Tendenz*] is no longer a deeply hidden element of art but rather has become completely flagrant. And this finally brings us to the film." (The manuscript breaks off here.)

Bartram has in his office. I was very struck by a long, narrow, rectangular wall map that allegorically represents history as a series of streams, sinuous bands of different colors. The names and dates were recorded in each stream bed in chronological order. The map was done at the beginning of the nineteenth century, I would have dated it one hundred and fifty years earlier. Next to it was an interesting mechanical clock, a landscape hanging on the wall in a glass case. The mechanism was broken and the clock whose strokes had once set into motion windmills, water wheels, window shutters, and human figures now no longer functioned. To the right and left of this, also under glass, similar reliefs were hanging — the sack of Troy, Moses making the water gush forth from the rock — but they were stationary. Besides all this there were children's books, a collection of playing cards, and a variety of other things. The museum was closed that day (Thursday) and the way to Bartram's office led through a courtyard which bordered on an especially beautiful old church. The variety of church steeple styles here is truly astounding. I assume that the narrow, delicate obelisk-shaped spires date from the eighteenth century. These churches rise above the courtyards very much the way that village churches emerge from a landscape occupied by few other buildings. I immediately went home afterwards to drop off a huge plate — a rare broadsheet, somewhat damaged and unfortunately glued to a cardboard backing, which Bartram had presented to me since he already had a duplicate of it in his collection. Then off to Reich's. Asja and Manya had just arrived (it was only during the following visit that I would make the acquaintance of the charming Dasha, a Ukrainian Jewess who was at that point doing Reich's cooking). The atmosphere was charged when I entered, and it took some effort on my part to avoid having it erupt against me. I sensed what had provoked it, but the reasons were so trivial I had no desire to remember them. And, predictably, things exploded between them shortly thereafter while Asja, sulky and irritable, was making Reich's bed. Finally we left. Asja was preoccupied with the various efforts she had been making to find a job, and she spoke of these on the way. In fact, we only walked together as far as the next streetcar stop. I was more or less hopeful about seeing her that evening, but first a telephone call would decide whether or not she would have to go see Knorin. I had become accustomed to setting as little store as possible in her promises. And when she called me up later to tell me that she was too tired to keep her appointment with Knorin, but that she had unexpectedly been informed by her seamstress that she had better go pick up her dress that very evening since nobody would be home the following day — her seamstress was checking into the hospital — I gave up all hope of seeing her that evening. But things worked out differently: Asja asked me to meet her in front of the seamstress's house and promised we would then go somewhere together after she was through. We had in mind one of the places on the Arbat. We arrived at the seamstress's house, which is next to the Theater of the Revolution, virtually at the same moment. Then I had to wait in front of it for nearly an hour — in the end I became

convinced that I had somehow missed Asja during the time I had briefly gone
to inspect one of the three courtyards of the house. For ten minutes I had been
telling myself that it was crazy to go on waiting like this, when she finally
emerged. We proceeded to the Arbat. And after a brief hesitation we went into
a restaurant by the name of Prague. We climbed the broad curved stairway that
led to the second floor and entered a brightly lit room with many tables, most of
which were unoccupied. To the right, at the other end of the room, was a stage
from which, at considerable intervals, there emanated orchestra music or the
voice of a lecturer or the songs of a Ukrainian choir. We changed tables right
off, Asja was feeling a draft from the window. She was embarrassed about having come to such a "refined" establishment wearing torn shoes. She had put on
her new dress at the seamstress's. It had been sewn together out of some old, already motheaten black fabric, but it looked very good on her and on the whole
resembled her blue one. We began by talking about Astachov. Asja ordered a
shashlyk and I had a glass of beer. We were sitting there face to face, musing
about my departure, looking at each other. At which point Asja told me, and it
was probably the first time she had been this open, that there had been a time
when she would have very much wanted to marry me. And if things had not
turned out that way, she thought it was I and not she who had gambled away
the opportunity. (Perhaps she didn't quite use a term as cutting as "gambled
away"; I no longer remember.) I said if she had wanted to marry me then her
demons had certainly played a role in this wish. ·— Yes, she had thought about
how unbelievably comical it would have been to introduce herself as my wife to
my acquaintances. But now, in the wake of her illness, she was free of her demons. She had become completely passive. But there was no more future in store
for us now. I: But I'm going to hold on to you, even if you go to Vladivostok,
I'll follow you there. — Do you want to go on playing the family friend with the
Red general as well? If he is as dumb as Reich and doesn't throw you out of the
house, I have nothing against it. And if he does throw you out, I have nothing
against that either. — At another point she said, "I have already gotten so used
[to you]." — But in the end I said, "The first days after my arrival here I told
you I was ready to marry you immediately. But I don't really know if I could go
through with it. I think I wouldn't be able to stand it." And then she said something quite beautiful: Why not? I'm a faithful dog. When I live with a man I
adopt a barbarous attitude — it is of course wrong, but I can't do anything
about it. If you were with me, you wouldn't go through all the anxiety and sadness that so often comes over you. — We went on talking in this fashion. Was I
going to go on always looking at the moon and thinking of Asja? I said that I
hoped things would have improved by the next time we saw each other. — You
mean you'll be fit enough again to be at me twenty-four hours out of the day? —
I said this was not exactly what I had had in mind, I was only thinking of being
closer to her, of talking to her. Only if I were closer to her would this other desire then return. "How lovely," she said. — This conversation left me very un-

settled all the following day, and even throughout the night. But my wish to travel had in fact been more powerful than my desire for her, even though this may very well have only been due to the many obstacles the latter had encountered. Just as it continues to encounter them now. Life in Russia is too difficult for me within the Party and there are far fewer prospects outside of it, though life is hardly less difficult. She, on the other hand, has put down a number of roots here in Russia. Then again there is, of course, her nostalgia for Europe, which is closely connected to what she might find attractive about me. And to live in Europe with her — this could one day become the most important, the most tangible thing for me, if only she could be won over to it. In Russia — I have my doubts. We took a sleigh back to her apartment, hugged closely together. It was dark. This was the only moment in the dark that we had shared in Moscow — out in the middle of the street, on the narrow seat of a sleigh.

January 28. Ventured forth early into the glorious thaw in order to explore the streets to the right of the Arbat as I had long intended to do. I thus arrived at the square where the kennel of the czars had formerly stood. It is formed by low houses, some of which have portals supported by columns. But standing among these on one side are some hideous tall buildings that are newer. The "Museum of Daily Life in the Forties" is located here — a low, three-story house whose rooms have been very tastefully maintained in the style of a rich bourgeois household of the period. It contains beautiful furniture with many reminiscences of the Louis Philippe style, chests, candlesticks, pier glasses, folding screens (one very unusual one with thick glass between its wood panels). All the rooms have been arranged as if they were still inhabited, paper, notes, dressing gowns, shawls lie on the tables or hang over the chairs. In fact it takes almost no time to walk through the whole thing. To my astonishment, there was no actual children's room to be found (and thus no toys). Perhaps playrooms did not exist back then? Or was it missing? Or was it located on the locked uppermost floor? Then I walked around the sidestreets some more. Finally I found myself back on the Arbat, stopped at a bookstall and discovered a book by Victor Tissot published in 1882, *La Russie et les Russes.* I bought it for twenty-five kopeks, thinking it might just provide me with some facts and names that could help me get an idea of Moscow and be of use for the article on the city I was planning. I dropped the book off at home and went to see Reich. Our conversation went more smoothly this time; I had sworn to myself that I would not let any tension develop. We talked about *Metropolis*[164] and its poor reception in Berlin, at least among the intellectuals. Reich laid the responsibility for this failed experiment squarely on the shoulders of those intellectuals whose exaggerated expectations prompted these kinds of hazardous enterprises. I disagreed. Asja did not show

164. 1926 film by Fritz Lang (1890–1976).

up — she would appear that evening. But Manya was there for a while. And Dasha was also in the room — a small Ukrainian Jewess who lives there and now cooks for Reich. I found her quite attractive. The girls were speaking Yiddish but I could not make out what they were saying. When I got back home, I called up Asja and asked her to drop by on her way back from Reich's. Which she actually did. She was very tired and immediately lay down on the bed. I was at first quite embarrassed and could barely get a word out of my throat for fear of seeing her immediately get up and leave. I got out the big mousy broadsheet that Bartram had given me and showed it to her. Then we discussed Sunday: I promised I would of course accompany her out to see Daga. We kissed again and spoke of living together in Berlin, of getting married, of taking at least one trip together. Asja said that there had never been another city as difficult for her to leave as Berlin, did this have something to do with me? The two of us took a sleigh to Rachlin's. There was not enough snow on Tverskaia to allow the sleigh to proceed with any speed. Progress improved on the side streets: the driver took a route I was unfamiliar with, we passed by a bathhouse and saw a marvelous out-of-the-way corner of Moscow. Asja told me about Russian bathhouses; I already knew that they functioned as the actual centers of prostitution, just as they had in medieval Germany. I told her about Marseilles.[165] There were no visitors at Rachlin's place when we arrived there shortly before ten. It was a lovely, quiet evening. She told me all sorts of details about the archives. Among other things, that they had discovered that the ciphered passages in the correspondence between some of the members of the czar's family contained the most unspeakable pornography. A discussion as to whether this should be published or not. I realized the truth of Reich's insightful observation that Rachlin and Manya belonged to the category of "moralistic" communists who will always take a middle-of-the-road position and will never envisage the possibilities of a truly "political" one. I sat on the large couch, snuggled against Asja. Groats were served with milk and tea. I left around a quarter to eleven. Even at night the weather was wonderfully warm.

January 29. The day was a failure in almost every respect. I appeared at Basseches's place around eleven in the morning and unexpectedly found him already awake and working. But I had to wait around for him all the same. This time there was a delay because his mail had been misplaced; it took at least half an hour for it to be located. Then there was a wait for some typing to be finished and in the meantime I was as usual given some recently written editorials to read in manuscript. In short, the already difficult formalities of my departure were made even more unbearable by this way of dealing with them. Over the

---

165. Cf. Benjamin's comments on the red-light district in his 1928 essay "Marseilles," in *Reflections*, p. 131.

course of the day it became apparent that the advice Gnedin had given me about clearing my baggage through customs in Moscow was totally absurd. And when I later thought of him in the midst of all the unimaginable difficulties and complications he had gotten me into, my old travel maxim engraved itself even more deeply into my mind: never take the advice of anybody who has not been asked for it. The corollary of this of course is: when you put your affairs in somebody else's hands (as I had), you must strictly follow their advice. But Basseches nonetheless left me in the lurch on the final crucial day of my departure, and on February 1, a few hours before I was due to leave, it took an incredible effort on my part, and the help of the servant he had sent along with me, to get my trunk expedited. Almost nothing got accomplished that morning. We retrieved the passport and the exit visa from the militia. It did not occur to me in time that it was Saturday and that it was unlikely that the customs office would be open after one o'clock. When we finally got to the Narkomindel [166] it was after two, for we had leisurely sauntered down Petrovka on foot, had then stopped at the administrative building of the Bolshoi Theater where Basseches used his influence to reserve two ballet tickets for me for Sunday, and finally had gone to the state bank. When we finally got to Kalanchevskaia Square around two-thirty, we were informed that the customs officials had just left. I got into an automobile with Basseches and asked to be dropped off at a streetcar stop so I could proceed on to Rachlin's. Plans had been made for me to drop by and pick her up at two-thirty before going out to the Lenin hills together. Both she and Asja were home. Asja did not respond as enthusiastically as I had expected to my announcement that I had procured tickets for the ballet. She said it would have been wiser to get tickets for Monday, when *The Inspector General* was scheduled to be performed at the Bolshoi Theater. I was so exhausted and irritated by the futile exertions of the morning that I didn't even bother to reply. Meanwhile Rachlin invited me to have dinner there after we had returned from our excursion. I accepted, having made sure that Asja would still be there. But our little expedition turned out as follows: not far from the house a streetcar literally passed right under our noses. We continued in the direction of Revolution Square — Rachlin probably thought it would be better to wait there because there were more streetcar lines from which to choose. But I'm not sure. It was not the walking that I found fatiguing, rather the conversation with all its innuendos and misunderstandings had so worn me down that it was out of sheer feebleness that I said yes when she asked me if we should hop on a streetcar that happened to be passing by. Admittedly, I had made the error of calling her attention to this streetcar with my eyes, otherwise she wouldn't have noticed it. She was already standing on its platform and it was gradually picking up speed, so I ran alongside it for a few steps but did not hop on. She

166. Abbreviation of Narodnyi komissariat inostrannykh del (People's Committee on Foreign Affairs).

shouted to me "I'll wait [for] you there," and I slowly made my way across Red Square to the streetcar stop in its middle. She must have only waited for me there for a short time because when I arrived she was nowhere to be found. I stood there, unable to figure out where she could have disappeared to. Finally I decided she must have meant she was going to wait for me at the end of the line, so I got on the next streetcar and took it to the last stop, riding for about half an hour in a more or less straight path through that part of town that lies on the far side of the Moskva. At bottom, I may very well have deliberately contrived to take this solitary ride. The fact is that any excursion I might have taken with her, no matter where it might have led, would have been far less enjoyable. I wouldn't have had the strength for it. But now I was feeling quite contented with this forced, nearly pointless trip through a part of the city with which I was completely unfamiliar. For the first time I noticed the absolute similarity between certain parts of the outskirts and the harbor streets of Naples. I also saw the enormous Moscow radio transmitter, whose shape is different from any other I have seen. On the right side of the avenue that the streetcar was following, there were occasional mansions, on the left side were scattered sheds or cottages, open field for the most. The village character of Moscow suddenly leaps out at you undisguisedly, evidently, unambiguously in the streets of its suburbs. There is probably no other city whose gigantic open spaces have such an amorphous, rural quality, as if their expanse were always being dissolved by bad weather, thawing snow, or rain. The streetcar line ended in front of an inn situated in one of these expanses that was no longer urban and yet not quite rural either, and of course Rachlin was not there. I immediately took a streetcar back into town, having just enough energy left to make it back home rather than accepting her invitation to dinner. Instead of lunch, I ate a few of the local waffles. I had barely gotten home when Rachlin called up. I was annoyed with her for no good reason and more or less on the defensive, so I was all the more pleasantly surprised by her friendly, soothing words. Above all they indicated to me that she would not convey the incident to Asja in a completely ridiculous light. But I declined her invitation to come right over for dinner; I was simply too tired. We arranged it that I would drop by around seven. I was most pleasantly surprised to find myself alone with her and Asja. I no longer remember what we talked about. The only thing I recall is that as I was leaving — Rachlin had already left the room — Asja blew me a kiss. Then a futile attempt to get something warm to eat in a restaurant on the Arbat. I wanted to order soup and they brought me two small slices of cheese.

January 30. I am adding certain things about Moscow that have only occurred to me here in Berlin (where, since the 5th of February, I have been continuing these notes, starting with the January 29 entry). For someone who has arrived from Moscow, Berlin is a dead city. The people on the street seem desperately

Vladimir Fyodorovich Shukhov. Moscow Radio Tower. *1926.*

isolated, each one at a great distance from the next, all alone in the midst of a broad stretch of street. Furthermore: as I was traveling from the Zoo railway station toward the Grunewald, the neighborhood I had to cross struck me as scrubbed and polished, excessively clean, excessively comfortable. What is true of the image of the city and its inhabitants is also applicable to its mentality: the new perspective one gains on this is the most indisputable consequence of a stay in Russia. However little one might still know of Russia, one learns to observe and judge Europe with a conscious awareness of what is taking place in Russia. This is the first thing that is incumbent on the attentive European in Russia. It is moreover precisely for this reason that a stay in Russia is so exact a touchstone for the foreign visitor. It obliges everybody to choose and carefully define his point of view. In general, the more marginal, the more private, the more inadequate to the scope of the Russian experience this point of view is, the more it will lend itself to facile theorizing. When one penetrates more deeply into the Russian situation, one no longer feels oneself immediately driven to the abstractions that so effortlessly come to the European's mind. — During the final days of my stay it seemed to me that the Mongol peddlers with their color-ful paper goods were again in greater evidence. I saw a man — in fact not a Mongol but a Russian — who in addition to baskets was selling small cages made out of glazed paper and containing small paper birds. But I also came across a real parrot, a white macaw: on Miasnitskaia, sitting on a basket containing linen goods a woman was selling to passers-by. — Elsewhere I saw children's swings being sold on the street. Moscow has been virtually rid of the sound of bells that tends to spread such an irresistible sadness over large cities. This too is something one only realizes and appreciates upon one's return. — Asja was waiting for me when I arrived at Yaroslavsky station. I was late because I had had to wait for a streetcar for a quarter of an hour and because there were no buses on Sunday morning. There was no time now for breakfast. The day, or at least the morning, was accompanied by anxiety attacks. Only as we were driving back from the sanatorium did I come to enjoy fully the mag-nificent sleigh ride. The weather was quite mild, and the sun was at our backs; when I placed my hand on Asja's back I could even feel its warmth. Our *izvoshchik* was a son of the same man who always served as Reich's driver. This time I learned that the charming small houses along the way were not dachas but rather the homes of wealthy peasants. Asja was very happy on the drive out, so the shock was all the greater when she arrived. Daga was not outside with the other children who were playing in the warm sun in the thawing snow. They called for her inside. She came down the stone stairs to the lobby, her face tear-ful, her shoes and stockings torn, virtually barefoot. It turned out that she had never received the package with stockings that had been sent to her, and that no one had been looking after her at all for the past two weeks. Asja was so upset she could barely muster a word, and was unable to have it out with the doctor as she had intended. She spent practically the entire time sitting next to

Daga on a wooden bench in the entranceway, desperately mending the shoes and stockings. But later she even reproached herself for having tried to repair the shoes. They were slippers that were in such a sorry state that they could no longer keep the child warm. And she was afraid that she would now be forced to go on wearing them instead of being allowed to run around in shoes or *valenki*. We had originally planned to take a five-minute drive in the sleigh with Daga; but this proved impossible. All the other visitors had already left and Asja was still sitting there sewing when Daga was called to dinner. We left; Asja absolutely despondent. We arrived at the train station just a few minutes after the train had pulled out, so we had nearly a full hour's wait in front of us. At first we played the game "where shall we sit?" Asja had her mind set on a spot where I absolutely did not want to sit. But when she finally gave in, I remained obstinate and insisted on the first spot. We ordered some ham, eggs, and tea. On the way back I spoke of the dramatic idea that had been suggested to me by Illés's play: to stage the story of a convoy during the Revolution (carrying, say, provisions destined for prisoners). We took a sleigh from the railway station to go see Reich, who had in the meantime moved into new quarters. The following day Asja would in turn move in. We spent a very long time up there while waiting for the meal. Reich again questioned me about the essay on humanism, and I explained to him that in my opinion one had to pay particular attention to the fact that the distinction between the scholar and the man of letters — two types which had once been identical (or at least unified in the person of the scholar) — coincides with the essential victory of the bourgeoisie and the declining position of the man of letters. It is worth noting that during the period that prepared the Revolution, the most influential men of letters were no less scholars than they were poets. Indeed, there may very well have been a preponderance of scholars. I was beginning to get one of the back aches that kept on plaguing me during my last days in Moscow. Finally the meal arrived, brought to us by a neighbor. It was very good. Asja and I then left, each going home our separate ways, to meet later that evening at the ballet. We passed by a drunk lying on the street smoking a cigarette. I put Asja on a streetcar and then made my way back to the hotel, where I found the theater tickets waiting. That evening they were performing Stravinsky's *Petrushka, Les Sylphides* — a ballet by an unimportant composer [167] — and Rimsky-Korsakov's *Capriccio Espagnol.* I arrived early and, aware this was the last night in Moscow I could talk to Asja in private, I waited for her in the lobby, hoping only that I would be able to go into the theater early with her and just sit there for a long time waiting for the curtain to rise. Asja arrived late, but we were still able to get to our seats just in time. Some Germans were sitting behind us; in our row there was a Japanese couple with two daughters, who were wearing their gleaming black hair Japanese-

---

167. *Les Sylphides* (original Russian title, *Chopiniana*), music by Chopin arranged by A. Glasunov (who must be the "unimportant composer").

style. We were sitting seven rows back from the stage. The second ballet featured the celebrated though now aged ballerina Gelzer, whom Asja had known in Orel.[168] *Les Sylphides* is a silly ballet in many respects, but it gives an excellent idea of the style this theater used to have. The piece probably dates back to the days of Nicholas I. It provides the kind of entertainment that one gets out of parades. As a finale, the magnificently staged Rimsky-Korsakov ballet, rushing by at the speed of wind. There were two intermissions. During the first one, I left Asja on her own and went out to try to get a program in front of the theater. When I returned I saw her leaning against a wall, engaged in conversation with a man. I realized with horror how insultingly I had stared at him, when I later learned from Asja that it had been Knorin. He always addresses her in the familiar *Du* — so insistently that she has little choice but to respond to him in the same form. When he asked her whether she was at the theater alone, she had replied, no, she was here with a journalist from Berlin. She had previously mentioned me to him. That evening Asja was wearing the new dress for which I had provided the fabric. Around her shoulders she was wearing the yellow wrap that I had brought from Rome to Riga for her. Since the color of her face, partly by nature, partly on account of her illness and the stress of the day, was also a yellow in which there was not the slightest trace of red, her entire appearance consisted of the gradations between three closely neighboring colors. After the theater I had only time to discuss the following evening with her. Since I was going to be away all day if I really wanted to make the excursion to Troitse,[169] only the evening remained. But she wanted to stay home because she was intending to drive out to see Daga again early the following morning. So we left it that I would definitely come see her in the evening, although we reached this agreement only at the very last moment. In the middle of our discussion, Asja wanted to hop on a streetcar — but decided not to. We were standing in the hustle and bustle of the large square in front of the theater. Animosity and love were shifting within me like winds; finally we said good-bye, she from the platform of the streetcar, I remaining behind, debating whether or not to follow her, leap after her.

January 31. My departure was now irrevocably fixed for the 1st by the reservation I had made on the 30th. But I still had to get my trunk cleared through customs. As agreed, I appeared at Basseches's place at a quarter of eight so that we would have time enough to go to the customs office and then catch the train at ten. In reality, the train didn't leave until ten-thirty. But we didn't discover

---

168.   Ekaterina Gelzer (1876–1952), noted ballerina who danced in the Moscow Bolshoi Theater from 1898–1934; she was designated in 1925 the first "people's artist of the RSFSR." Asja Lacis did experimental children's theater in Orel in 1918–1919.
169.   The Troitse-Sergeieva monastery in Sergeiev (renamed Zagorsk in 1930).

this in time enough to make use of the extra half hour. In fact, it was thanks to this delay that our excursion to Troitse took place at all. Had the train indeed left at ten, we would have certainly missed it. The formalities at the customs office were painfully drawn out and we were unable to get matters settled that day. Naturally I again had to pay for a taxi. The entire endeavor proved to be unnecessary since they didn't even take notice of the toys, which would certainly also have been the case at the border. The servant had come along to retrieve my passport here at the customs office and then immediately take it over to the Polish consulate to pick up my visa. So: not only did we make the train but we had to wait in it for twenty minutes before it pulled out. I told myself, not without annoyance, that we could have been settling the customs procedures in the meantime. But since Basseches was already in a fairly bad mood, I kept this to myself. The trip was monotonous. I had forgotten to bring any reading along and slept part of the way. Two hours later we reached our destination. I had still not mentioned my intention to buy some toys here. I was afraid he might reach the end of his patience. As chance would have it, our very first steps took us by a toy shop, so I mentioned what I had in mind. But I was reluctant to drag him into the store right off. The large fortresslike monastery complex rose before us on a slight elevation. The sight was far grander than I had expected. Closed in upon itself like a fortified city, it could remind one of Assisi; but strangely enough it was Dachau[170] that first came to my mind: its hill, crowned with a church, rises above the city just as the church here emerges from the midst of long rows of buildings. Things were fairly dead that day: all the various tailor, watchmaker, baker, cobbler shops that lie at the foot of the monastery hill were closed. Here, too, the winter weather was extremely beautiful and warm, though the sun was not out. The sight of the toy shop had put my desire to make some purchases here very much at the fore of my mind, and I was therefore impatient to get through the visit to the monastery's treasures; I was acting exactly like the kind of tourist no one hates more than I do. Our guide, the administrator of the museum that had been created out of the monastery, was all the more pleasant. But there were other reasons as well for my impatience. It was freezing cold in most of the rooms through which a servant preceded us, removing the coverings of the glass cases in which the priceless tapestries, the articles of gold and silver, the manuscripts, the devotional objects were displayed; and it was probably during this one-hour tour that I caught the terrible cold that I came down with upon my return to Berlin. In the end the infinite quantity of precious objects, whose actual artistic value can for the most only be discerned by specialists or connoisseurs, exercises a numbing effect on you, indeed it brutalizes the eye. In addition, Basseches was intent on seeing "everything" there was to be seen and even asked to be escorted down to the crypt, where the bones of St. Sergius, the founder of this monastery, lie under

170. Benjamin spent several months in Dachau in 1917 undergoing treatment for his sciatica.

glass. It is impossible for me to enumerate, even partially, everything there was to be seen. Leaning against a wall was the famous Rublev icon that has become the symbol of this monastery. Later, when we were visiting the cathedral, we saw the empty spot in the iconostasis where the painting had hung before being removed for restoration. The mural paintings in the cathedral are seriously threatened. Since central heating is not used, the walls warm up abruptly in the spring, causing cracks and fissures through which the dampness seeps. In a closet I saw the enormous metal casing, entirely incrusted with precious stones, that was subsequently intended for the Rublev icon. The only parts of the angels' bodies that are left undecorated are those without clothes: the faces and the hands. Everything else is covered with a thick layer of gold, and when the template is placed over the painting the necks and arms of the angels, bound as it were in heavy metal chains, must give them the appearance of Chinese criminals expiating their crimes in neck-irons. The tour ended in the room where our guide lived. The old man had been married, for he pointed out the oil portraits of his wife and daughter that were hanging on the walls. But now he lives alone in this large, bright, monkish room, not entirely cut off from the world because many foreigners visit the monastery. On a small table there was an opened package of scholarly books that had just arrived from England. And here, too, we signed the guest book. Even among the bourgeoisie this custom seems to have survived far longer in Russia than here, at least to judge from the fact that Schick also presented me with an album to sign. — But the actual layout of the monastery was even grander than anything it held. We had stopped in front of the portal before making our way into the large space enclosed by fortificationlike structures. Two bronze plaques to the right and the left were inscribed with what was known of the essential dates concerning the history of the monastery. More beautiful and simpler than the yellowish pink rococo-style church that rises in the middle of the courtyard surrounded by smaller, older buildings — among which the mausoleum of Boris Godunov[171] — are the long farm buildings and living quarters that form a rectangle around the enormous open square. The most beautiful of them all, the large brightly colored refectory. The view from its windows includes both this square as well as ditches, passageways between walls, a labyrinth of stone fortifications. There was also once an underground passage here which two monks blew up, at the cost of their own lives, to save the monastery during the siege. We ate in a *stolovaia* that was located in the courtyard of the monastery, diagonally across from the entrance. *Zakuski*, vodka, soup, and meat. Several large rooms filled with people, with many real Russian village, or rather small town, types — since Sergeievo has recently been declared a town. As we were eating, a peddler came by hawking wire racks that could be instantly transformed from a lampshade into a plate or a fruit container. Basseches was of the opinion that they

---

171. Boris Godunov (1552–1605), legendary Russian czar.

came from Croatia. I myself felt a memory from the very distant past stir within me as I caught sight of these rather ugly playthings. My father must have bought something of this sort during some summer vacation (at Freudenstadt?) when I was very young. During the meal Basseches asked the waiter for the addresses of the local toy shops and then we proceeded on our way. We had barely been walking for ten minutes when Basseches briefly stopped for directions, which led us to turn back and grab an empty sleigh that happened to be passing by. The walk after the meal had taxed my energies, so I didn't even want to inquire what had caused us to turn back. But this much was clear: the shops near the railway station were where we would be most likely to find what I wanted. There were two of them, not far from each other. The first one contained articles made of wood. Since it was already getting dark, they turned on the lights for us when we came in. As I had expected, a shop featuring wooden toys could not offer me much with which I was not already familiar. I bought a few items, more at Basseches's insistence than out of any decision of my own, but I am now happy that I did so. Here, too, we lost time, I had to wait ages before we managed to get a *chervonets* changed in the neighborhood. I was burning with impatience to get to the shop with the papier-mâché toys; I was afraid it might already have closed. Which was not the case. But when we got there at long last, the house was already completely dark inside and there was no lighting in the storeroom. We had to feel our way around the shelves at random. Now and then I would light a match. In this way a number of very beautiful items came into my hands which probably wouldn't have happened otherwise since we were obviously unable to make it clear to the man what it was I was looking for. When we finally got back into the sleigh, each of us had two large packages — in addition, Basseches had a mass of brochures he had bought at the monastery in order to gather material for an article. The long wait in the depressingly lit railway station restaurant was alleviated by more tea and *zakuski*. I was tired and beginning to feel sick. This was not unrelated to my anxiety about all the things I still had to settle in Moscow. The trip back was picturesque. There was in our car a lit lantern whose stearin candle got stolen in the course of the trip. Not far from our seats was an iron stove. Strewn haphazardly under the benches were large logs. Now and then one of the employees would go to a seat, lift it up, and remove further fuel from the chest he had opened. It was eight when we got into Moscow. This was my last evening, Basseches got a taxi. I asked him to have it wait in front of my hotel while I dropped off the toys I had bought and hastily gathered together the manuscripts I was supposed to deliver to Reich in an hour. At Basseches's place, protracted instructions to his servant, whom I promised to pick up around eleven-thirty. Then I took a streetcar and luckily guessed right about the stop I had to get off at to reach Reich's apartment, so I got there earlier than I had expected. I would have gladly taken a sleigh, but it would have been impossible: I neither knew the name of the street on which Reich lived, nor was I able to locate the name of the neighboring square on the city map. Asja was already in bed. She said she had waited up for me for a long time but then had no longer counted on my arrival. [She] had wanted to take me out immediately to show me a seedy bar that she had discovered by chance right here in the neighborhood. There was also a bathhouse nearby. She had come across all of this in the course of getting lost and finding her way back here through courtyards and side alleys. Reich was also in the room, he was beginning to grow a beard. I was extremely worn out, so much so that, explicitly pleading my utter exhaustion, I reacted somewhat crudely to some of Asja's usual nervous inquiries (about her little sponge, etc.). But things were going very quickly. I told them about my excursion as best I could, given the brief time available. Then came the messages to be delivered in Berlin: telephone calls to a wide variety of acquaintances. Later Reich left the room to listen to the radio rebroadcast of the production of *The Inspector General* starring Chekhov[172] at the Bolshoi Theater, thus leaving me alone with Asja for a while. Asja was planning to drive out to see Daga the following morning, so I had to take into account the possibility that I might not see her again before my departure. When Reich returned, Asja went into the next room to listen to the radio. I didn't stay very much longer. But before I left I showed the postcards I had brought back from the monastery.

February 1. I once again went to my pastry shop that morning, ordered coffee and ate a sweet roll. Then to the toy museum. Not all the photos I had ordered were ready. I didn't mind because it meant I was being refunded ten *chervonets* at a moment when I badly needed the money. (I had paid for the photographs in advance.) I only spent a brief time at the toy museum, then raced over to the Kameneva Institute to say good-bye to Dr. Nieman. From there via sleigh to Basseches's. From there to the ticket office with his servant, and then by taxi to the customs office. What I again had to go through there defies description. There was a twenty-minute wait in front of a cashier's window while banknotes were being counted by the thousands. No one in the entire place was willing to change five rubles. It was absolutely imperative that my trunk, which not only contained all my beautiful toys but also all my manuscripts, leave by the same train for which I had a ticket. Since it could not be checked through further than the border, it was essential that I be there when it arrived. This was finally arranged. But once again I had to witness the extent to which servility still runs in people's blood here — the servant was totally defenseless against all the chicanery and lethargy of the customs officials. I breathed more easily when I was at last able to send him on his way with a *chervonets*. All the agitation had brought on my back pains again. I was glad to have a few peaceful hours ahead of me. I dawdled down the beautiful row of booths in the square, bought another pouch

172. Mikhail Alexandrovich Chekhov (1891–1955), actor and director, emigrated in 1928.

of Crimean tobacco, and ordered lunch in the restaurant of Yaroslavsky railway station. I still had enough money to telegraph Dora and buy a domino set for Asja. I brought my full powers of attention to bear on these final errands in the city; and they gave me pleasure because I was able to let myself go in a way that had not usually been the case during the period of my stay. I was back at the hotel shortly before three. The Swiss told me that a woman had been by. She had said she would be back. I went to my room and then straight up to the office to pay my bill. It was only when I got back to my room that I noticed a note from Asja on the table. It said she had been waiting for me for a long time, had not eaten, and was in the nearby *stolovaia*. I was to meet her there. I rushed down to the street and saw her coming in my direction. She had only had a piece of meat to eat and was still hungry, and before taking her back to my room I ran out into the square and bought her some tangerines and snacks. In my haste I had taken my room key with me; Asja was waiting in the lobby. I said, "Why didn't you just go into the room? The key is in the door." And I was struck by the rare friendliness of her smile when she said "No." She had found Daga in good shape this time and had engaged in a bitter but fruitful exchange of views with the doctor. Now she was lying on the bed in my room, wan, but feeling well. I sat by her side, then moved to the table, where I wrote my address on envelopes for her, then went to my suitcase and unpacked the toys I had purchased during the past few days and showed them to her. She took a great deal of pleasure in this. But in the meantime — not without cause, and also on account of my utter exhaustion — I was fighting back tears. We discussed a few more things. How I should or shouldn't write her. I asked her to make a tobacco pouch for me. To write. Finally, since there were only a few minutes left, my voice began to falter and Asja noticed that I was crying. At last she said to me: Don't cry, or else I'll end up crying myself and once I get started, I can't stop as easily as you can. We held each other tight. Then we went up to the office, where there was nothing to be taken care of (but I didn't want to wait for the Sovietdushi), the maid appeared — I slipped away from her without giving her a tip, and made my way out of the hotel with Asja following me with Reich's coat under her arm. I asked her to hail a sleigh. As I was about to get in, having said good-bye to her one more time, I invited her to ride to the corner of Tverskaia with me. I dropped her off there, and as the sleigh was already pulling away, I once again drew her hand to my lips, right in the middle of the street. She stood there a long time, waving. I waved back from the sleigh. At first she seemed to turn around as she walked away, then I lost sight of her. Holding my large suitcase on my knees, I rode through the twilit streets to the station in tears.

Nineteenth-century dollhouse furniture made by convicts in Siberia.

Painted wooden toy representing the earth on three whales. Motif derived from Russian legend.

Carved wooden toy from the Vladimir province, ca. 1860–1870.

Appendices

Russian Toys*

The toys of all cultures were products, initially, of a cottage industry. The stock of primitive forms in use by the lower groups in society, the peasants and the artisans, provided the sure foundation for the development of children's toys up to the present. There is nothing remarkable about this. The spirit from which these products emanate—the entire process of their production and not merely its result—is alive for the child in the toy, and he naturally understands a primitively produced object much better than one deriving from a complicated industrial process. Herein, incidentally, lies the legitimate basis of the modern trend to produce "primitive" children's toys. If only our artisans would not so often forget when doing this that it is not the constructive, schematic forms that appear primitive to the child, but rather the total construction of his doll or his toy dog, insofar as he can imagine how it is made. This is just what he wants to know; this first establishes his vibrant relationship with toys. Precisely because of this, one could say, perhaps, that only the Germans and the Russians, of all Europeans, possess the real genius for making toys.

The German toy industry is the most international. The tiny doll and animal kingdoms, the matchbox farmhouse rooms, the Noah's arks, and the sheep pens as they are made in the villages of Thuringia and the Erzgebirge, as well as in the Nuremberg region, are universally known, not only in Germany, but throughout the entire world. On the other hand, Russian toys are generally unknown. Their production is barely industrialized and they are hardly disseminated beyond the Russian borders, except for the stereotyped figure of the "Baba," the cone-shaped piece of wood, that, painted over and over again, represents a peasant woman.

In fact Russian toys are the finest, most diversified of all. The 150 million people who inhabit the country are composed of hundreds of nationalities, and all of these in turn have a more or less primitive, more or less accomplished artistic skill. Thus toys are produced in hundreds of different stylistic idioms, of the most diverse materials. Wood, clay, bone, textiles, paper, papier-mâché appear alone or in combinations. Wood is the most important among these materials. There is an incomparable mastery of its handling—of carving, coloring, and lacquering—almost everywhere in this land of great forests. From the simple jumping-jacks of soft, white willowwood; from the lifelike carved cows, pigs, and sheep to the lacquered jewelry caskets on which the peasant in his *troika*, countryfolk gathered around a samovar, women harvesters, or woodcutters at

*   This essay, translated by Gary Smith, first appeared as "Russische Spielsachen," in the *Südwestdeutsche Rundfunkzeitung*; it was reprinted in *GS*, III, pp. 623–625. On his working copy of the published text, Benjamin noted "abridged text, see manuscript." The original manuscript, however, is not among his papers. All that is known is that Benjamin sent to the *Rundfunkzeitung* eleven photographs, of which only six were published (*GS*, III, pp. 1051–1052).

Doll made of straw, traditionally associated with the summer harvest.

Samovar Christmas-tree ornament and mechanical toy drummer.

work are artfully painted with glowing colors; to huge groups of monsters, sculptured renderings of old sagas and legends — wooden toys, wooden gadgets fill shop after shop in the most elegant streets of Moscow, Leningrad, Kiev, Kharkov, and Odessa. The Moscow Toy Museum owns the largest collection. Three cabinets of the museum are filled with clay toys from northern Russia. The robust rural expression of these dolls from the Viatka district stands in contrast to their highly fragile condition. They have, nevertheless, survived the long journey. And it is good that they have found a safe asylum in the Moscow museum. For who knows how long even this kind of folk art can withstand the triumphant progress of technology which today sweeps across Russia. Already the demand for these things has supposedly died, at least in the cities. But in the farmhouse the clay is still kneaded at day's end, painted with glowing colors, and fired; in their homeland, surely, these toys still live on.

Moscow
December 10, 1926

Dear Gerhard [Scholem],[1]

I am taking advantage of an unexpected half hour at my disposal in order to give you some news of myself at long last. By a rather curious coincidence, I believe that your brother is here in Moscow as well; from what I gathered yesterday, he has been invited to the extended session of the Comintern here as one of the representatives of the German "opposition."[2] Let me immediately reassure you by making it clear that I am not here on any official mission. But naturally I am finding out a great deal about things that are quite useful and interesting for me to know. My primary source of information is my friend Dr. Reich, who has been working here for a year, primarily as a theater critic for Russian newspapers. I arrived here on the 6th after a two-day trip and my days are so filled with things I see and hear that I go to bed half dead in the evening. Naturally this also has to do as much with my ignorance of Russian and with the cold as it does with the power of the impressions. I am still not sure how long I'll be staying here. Since my book is finally going to be published by Rowohlt, I can't stay away from Berlin forever. (The only thing that is coming out for Christmas is a volume of the Proust translation, which will immediately be sent to you.) I was very happy that you mailed me your wife's articles. Both the lovely and acute review of the novel as well as the note on Dorothea Schlegel gave me great pleasure. Shortly before leaving Berlin, I spoke with Mirjam Höflich.[3] — For the moment don't expect any attempt on my part to describe my stay here. I have not been here long enough and too many other things are demanding my attention. The best thing really would be to see each other in Paris next year so we could talk about this and other things.[4] In the meantime keep me abreast of your doings and send me what you are publishing. A brief note of mine, "Gruss in Marseilles," should be appearing shortly.[5] The things

1. Letter provided by the Department of Manuscripts, Jewish National Library, Hebrew University of Jerusalem.
2. Werner Scholem (1895–1940) was a Communist deputy in the German Reichstag. He helped form a left-oppositional splinter group within the KPD (along with Ruth Fischer, Arkady Maslow, and others), and in 1927 was expelled from the KPD during its Stalinization, though he remained a member of the Reichstag. He died in Buchenwald.
3. Mirjam Ben-Gavriel (1898–1980), actress, originally Austrian, who emigrated to Palestine in 1925 and was at this point visiting Berlin.
4. Benjamin and Scholem met in Paris at the end of April 1927, while Scholem was en route to London. This was their first meeting in four years, and there were to be only two more encounters prior to Benjamin's death in 1940. Their correspondence is immense; see Walter Benjamin and Gershom Scholem, *Briefwechsel 1933–1940*, Frankfurt, Suhrkamp, 1980. An English translation is forthcoming from Schocken.
5. "Les cahiers du Sud" appeared in the *Literarische Welt* on March 18, 1927; cf. *GS*, IV, pp. 483–485.

I'm doing for the *Literarische Welt* no doubt are reaching you at any rate — so here is Russia, for real. In the difficult, harsh living conditions of this winter, you never lose consciousness of just how remote from everything this metropolis (two and a half to three million inhabitants) is. Politically, this population figure certainly translates into an extraordinarily powerful dynamic factor, but from the point of view of civilization it becomes a force of nature that is difficult to control. The cost of living here is unimaginably high and has come as a truly disagreeable surprise to me, especially because I lend so little credence to the tales of professional "travelers" or "reporters." If one knows a bit of Russian and devotes one's entire time to work, one can make a fairly good living. As I think I already wrote you, I am doing some work for the official *Soviet Encyclopedia* and I am planning, among other things, to write a few articles for it. For the moment, I'm not going to publish anything in the newspapers. At any rate, Buber (!) has commissioned a long piece on Moscow for *Die Kreatur*.[6] This came about during his last visit to Berlin; he invited me to submit something and out of a variety of considerations I agreed to do so. This was around Hanukkah. I hope yours was a pleasant one. Dora and Stefan were doing well when I left. You'll probably be hearing from her directly that she has left Ullstein. And that she has become editor in chief at the *Praktische Berlinerin*,[7] which has been bought up by another firm. — The day before yesterday I spoke to Alexander Granovsky here, the director of a Jewish theater. Do you know of it? Tomorrow I am to meet with Kameneva (Trotsky's sister); she handles foreign contacts. They want to arrange a lecture for me. I think there are even plans to interview me about my "Moscow impressions." All this thanks to the cold weather here, which at the moment has somewhat frozen up the flow of intellectuals. (I found out some curious details about Toller's visit here that came to such a sudden end.) What's new with the two of you? Please reply to my Berlin address. Also tell me what the chances are of your coming to Paris. I think I'll be there around March. Warmest greetings to you and Escha.[8]

Yours, Walter

---

6. *Die Kreatur*, a literary quarterly, was then edited by Buber, Joseph Wittig, and Viktor von Weizsäcker. Benjamin's trip to Moscow was financed in part with an advance from Buber. The piece produced for *Die Kreatur*, "Moscow," has been translated into English in *Reflections*, pp. 97–136. See Benjamin's letter to Buber on pp. 132–133 of this issue.
7. Little is known about Dora Benjamin's activities at Ullstein Verlag, since the publishing house's archive was destroyed during the war. After 1927 the *Praktische Berlinerin* was renamed *Modenwelt*.
8. Elsa Burchardt Scholem was Gershom Scholem's first wife, from 1923–1936.

Moscow
Sadovaia Triumfalnaia
December 26, 1926

Dear Jula [Radt],[9]

    I hope you get this letter. If you do, write me a nice reply. If I am now venturing to write, it is because I have just had news from Germany for the first time since my arrival here. I had thought that all the letters were getting lost. But the mail seems to be reliable. I have already written you a postcard — Don't imagine that it is easy to report on things here. I will have to work a great deal on what I am seeing and hearing if I am to give it some sort of shape. In the current state of affairs, the present — even though it be fleeting — is of extraordinary value. Everything is being built or rebuilt and every moment poses very critical questions. The tensions of public life — which for the most part are actually of a theological sort — are so great that they block off all private life to an unimaginable degree. If you were here, you would probably be more astonished than I am; I remember some of the things you said about Russia at Agay during the summer.

    — I cannot assess all of this; basically, the situation here enables and requires one to take on a position within it, even though this might be a sceptical position in many respects; from the outside, all you can do is observe it. It is totally impossible to predict what's going to come of all this in Russia. Perhaps a truly socialist community, perhaps something entirely different. The battle that is going to decide this is still in progress. It is most productive to be in contact with this situation — but out of fundamental considerations it is impossible for me to get fully involved. It remains to be seen to what extent I'll be able to establish concrete relations with developments here. Various circumstances make it seem likely that from now on I will contribute substantial articles to Russian journals and it is possible that I might do considerable work for the *Encyclopedia.* There is much to be done and there is an unbelievable dearth of contributors competent in the humanities. — Beyond this, I am not yet sure what I am going to write about my stay here. I think I already mentioned to you that I have gathered a great amount of material together in the shape of a diary. — The lovely hum of a samovar allowed me to escape my terror of Christmas Eve. There have been many beautiful things: a sleigh ride through the Russian winter woods to visit a pretty little girl in a first-rate children's clinic. I have been going to the theater a great deal — about which there are incredible misconceptions abroad. To tell the truth, of all the plays I have seen so far, only Meyerhold's production is of real importance. Despite the freezing cold (down to [minus]

9.   Jula Radt (b. 1894) was for many years, especially from 1912–1915 and from 1921–1933, very close to Benjamin. She was a sculptor who from 1916–1922 was connected with the Stefan George circle; thereafter she returned to Berlin. She married Fritz Radt in 1925, and went to Holland in exile. Letter published in Benjamin, *Briefe,* pp. 439–441.

twenty-six degrees), it is quite pleasant to walk around the city, that is, if I am not too exhausted. Which is often the case because of my difficulties with the language and because of the rigors of daily life here. But a visit at this time of year is extremely good for my health and, when all is said and done, it's been a long time since I've felt this well. But things are unimaginably expensive here, Moscow may well be the most expensive place on earth. — I will fill you in more concretely on things when I get back. Did you get the head of me photographed by Stone? And how are you doing? Did Ilse[10] come to Berlin? How's Fritz? Write me a nice neat letter about all this using several sheets of your special onionskin stationery. You can address the letter to me in Roman letters. But answer me affectionately by return mail. I wish you pleasant demons for the new year.

Yours, Walter

[Postcard]

Dear Mr. Kracauer,[11]

I could offer many reasons for my long silence. Perhaps the best of which is provided by the close of your last letter: "But to *whom* does one write? Can you answer this?" Indeed, one could spend two months mulling over this question without coming up with an answer. But the fact of the matter is that I have been knocking around here for weeks, freezing on the outside, on fire inside — and I hope not in vain. But I barely have enough energy left over to do my day-to-day work. I will soon be returning. Please write me at Grunewald. At any rate, I would have been unable to give you any substantial report about things here because I must go on observing and reflecting up to the very last minute if I am in the end to come up with a halfway communicable summary of my stay — and even this could be little more than a small picture of Moscow. To tell the truth, one does not tire that easily of seeing this city. Have you spoken to Roth? He will have given you some articles for me and I would be most grate-

10.   Ilse Hermann was a friend of Jula Cohn-Radt, whose atelier was in the house of Hermann's parents.
11.   Siegfried Kracauer (1889–1966), novelist, critic, film theorist, whom Benjamin met through Ernst Bloch. Kracauer was a close friend of Joseph Roth and Theodor Adorno. From 1920–1933 he was a cultural affairs editor at the *Frankfurter Zeitung*, and through him Benjamin was able to place many reviews there. They corresponded extensively until around 1936. "Ornament der Masse" appeared in two parts in the *Frankfurter Zeitung* on July 9 and July 10, 1927, and was later reprinted as a chapter of a book by the same name (Frankfurt, Suhrkamp, 1963, pp. 50–63). This book included Kracauer's "Zu den Schriften Walter Benjamins," a review of Benjamin's *One-Way Street* and *Origin of German Tragic Drama*, one of only two substantial reviews of the former work. The postcard is in the collection of the Deutsches Literaturarchiv, Schiller Nationalmuseum, Marbach/Neckar.

ful if you could send them on to me at Grunewald. Hoping to find your own latest work (*Ornament der Masse*), etc., there upon my return, warm greetings

Yours, Walter Benjamin

Dr. W Benjamin
Moscow
Gost. "Tyrol"
Sadovaia Triumfalnaia
[January 1927]
I am saving your Kafka review so I can read it after I have familiarized myself with *The Castle*.

Dear Mr. Kracauer,[12]

j'ai été un peu long à vous ecrire. But upon my return I found there were many things I had to deal with in my little private toy editor's office; among which a flu. It's been a number of days now that I've been sifting through my "Moscow" dossier. You will perhaps come across some small notes of mine in the *Literarische Welt*. A lovely collection of photos (toys of Russian origin) should now have reached you in Frankfurt. I am offering them to the *Illustriertes Blatt*[13] and would have preferred to have asked you to act as the intermediary (since you will already have my text that is to accompany these pictures under your eyes), were it not for the fact that a friend took me *à l'improviste* to see [Karl] Otten, who has now sent them on to Frankfurt. Finally I am planning to write something "comprehensive" about Moscow. But as is so often the case with me, this will probably divide itself up into particularly small and disparate notes and for the most part the reader will be left to his own devices. But however it turns out and however much or little I manage to convey to my friends, these two months were a truly incomparable experience for me. To return richer in vivid perceptions than in theory — this had been my intent and I think I have profited by it. I see that I have thereby involuntarily moved closer to one of the characteristics of your Parisian notebooks, which in fact I enjoyed immensely. I dare say that my Paris "observations"[14] essentially coincide with yours. "The Luster of Affairs" — this is an absolutely outstanding formula of what it is that brings out the beauty of things and of life in this city, even under the harshest illumination. I don't know whether you've been following Gide's diary of his journey to Africa in the

---

12.   Letter provided by the Deutsches Literaturarchiv, Schiller Nationalmuseum, Marbach/Neckar.
13.   The photographs were ultimately published not in the *Illustriertes Blatt* of the *Frankfurter Zeitung* but in the *Südwestdeutsche Rundfunkzeitung*, vol. 6, no. 2 (January 19, 1930), p. 4. Benjamin wrote "Gekürzter Abdruck, s. Manuscript" ("abridged text, see manuscript") in his copy of the printed version. The manuscript, however, is not among his papers.
14.   Kracauer's "Pariser Beobachtungen" appeared in the *Frankfurter Zeitung* on February 13, 1927.

Nouvelle Revue Française. [15] But it is not surprising that the French governor was forced to resign on account of the things that have been reported (and in such unadulterated, severe fashion) about the French colonial atrocities there! Try to imagine the German parallel. Or better yet, draw on empirical experience and show me a single legal case since the election of Hindenburg that has punished child abuse with more than a fine or two weeks in jail. I hope we will soon be able to discuss this and related matters. I will be in Frankfurt for a few days in the middle of March. I very much hope to get together with you then. Which is why I am not going into greater detail here. In closing, let me specify several books listed in the *Büchereinlauf* which I would be interested in reviewing: Hamann, *Die Überseele — Grundzüge einer Morphologie der deutschen Literaturgeschichte*; Larissa Reissner, *Oktober* (both listed in no. 6); the *Doppelroman der berliner Romantik*, edited by Helmut Rogge (in no. 7); and finally Paul Hankamer's *Die Sprache Ihr Begriff und ihre Deutung im XVI. und XVII. Jahrhundert,* [16] which is announced in no. 8 and should be out in a few days. Since this is very close to my own field of work, it is important to me and I would especially appreciate the opportunity to review it. — Please let me hear from you. If you should see Ernst Bloch, could you please inform him that two letters I wrote to him from Moscow were returned as undeliverable and that I am anxious to have his address and to hear from him.
Warm greetings.

Yours, Walter Benjamin

February 23, 1927
Berlin-Grunewald
Delbrückstr. 23

[letter from Lunacharsky to the editors of the *Great Soviet Encyclopedia*] [17]

March 29, 1929

Dear comrades,

Please excuse me for having been so slow in reacting both to your letter and to the Goethe material you enclosed. Only now am I able to convey some sort of opinion on this matter to you.

I am in complete agreement with the evaluation of Benjamin's article that

---

15.   The diary was later published as *Voyage au Congo*, Paris, Gallimard (Editions de la Nouvelle Revue Française), 1927.
16.   Benjamin reviewed the last book, by Paul Hankamer (Bonn, F. Cohen, 1927), on July 15, 1927.
17.   Letter published in *Literaturnoe nasledstvo*, Moscow, 1970, vol. 82, pp. 534–535. An outstanding study of Lunacharsky's complex relations to German writers and literature is Dora Angres's *Die Beziehungen Lunacarskijs zur deutschen Literatur*, Berlin, Akademie, 1970.

is contained in the letter to the chief editor. This article is inappropriate, and not only on account of its nonencyclopedic character. It displays considerable talent and contains occasional insights that are surprisingly acute, but it draws no conclusions of any sort. What's more, he explains neither Goethe's place within European cultural history nor his place for us in — so to speak — our cultural pantheon. In addition, the contribution includes a number of extremely questionable theses.

I don't know whether you want to make use of this article, but I would in any event like to offer a few personal observations. The parenthesized passages on pages three and four should be omitted. One cannot let the statement on page five stand: "The German revolutionaries were not men of the Enlightenment, the German men of the Enlightenment were no revolutionaries." This totally fallacious assertion is later contradicted by the author himself when he speaks of the solid class viewpoint of Lessing, who was after all a man of the Enlightenment. On the same page the points concerning Goethe's aversion to any form of violent upheaval as well as to the state are very muddled, and absolutely no mention is made of the deeper reason for Goethe's hostility to Holbach's materialist worldview. On page six he then denies that Goethe's objection derived in large part from his own lucid sensitivity to the life of nature, a sensitivity that is extraordinarily close to the dialectical conception. The parenthesized portions of pages eight and nineteen should be omitted; I have in passing corrected a number of spelling and other errors. The idea expressed within parentheses on page fifty-nine is highly unclear. One can hardly agree with the author on page two of the second part that Goethe's conversations with Eckermann constitute one of the finest literary works of the nineteenth century.[18] The translator apparently left something out on page six; this passage should be restored.

All in all, I again recommend that Benjamin's article not be printed.

The article by Oskar Walzel is even less suitable.[19] It is of course extraordinarily difficult to seize Goethe's difficult and varied life in such a manner as to render justice to his diversity and even contradictoriness, while at the same time underscoring the profound unity that informs the life, the poetic and scientific works, etc., of Goethe. Despite the fact that Walzel claims to be merely elaborating, with a few corrections as it were, on Gundolf's work,[20] his article is not only ideologically unacceptable for a Marxist encyclopedia but also totally incoherent as a whole.

Not encouraging.

---

18.   See Johann Peter Eckermann, *Gespräche mit Goethe in den letzten Jahren seines Lebens*, Wiesbaden, Insel, 1963. An English edition is *Conversations with Eckermann*, New York, E. P. Dutton, 1935.
19.   See note 82.
20.   Friedrich Gundolf's *Goethe*, Berlin, George Bondi, 1916.

I can be of absolutely no help. The *Encyclopedia of Literature* decided to assign me the article on Goethe, and I was weak enough to accept. But in the meantime I have come to realize that given all my other commitments, it would be simply irresponsible on my part to undertake a task involving such responsibility.

Besides, the bibliography appended to Walzel's article is undoubtedly of value and certainly could be put to good use.

People's Committee on Public Instruction
[A. Lunacharsky]

Berlin
February 23, 1927

My esteemed Herr Buber,[21]

My visit to Moscow lasted somewhat longer than I had expected. And when I got back to Berlin, I then had to deal with a flu. I've been back at work for a few days now, but I will not be able to send you the manuscript before the end of February. Would you be so kind as to let me know when you are leaving Germany? I will make every attempt to get the manuscript into your hands at least eight days before your departure. The work by Wittig[22] you referred me to is valuable and illuminating. I can assure you of one thing with certainty — it is negative: my presentation will be devoid of all theory. In this fashion I hope to succeed in allowing the "creatural" to speak for itself: inasmuch as I have succeeded in seizing and rendering this very new and disorienting language that echoes loudly through the resounding mask of an environment that has been totally transformed. I want to write a description of Moscow at the present moment in which "all factuality is already theory" and which would thereby refrain from any deductive abstraction, from any prognostication, and even within certain limits, from any judgment — all of which, I am absolutely convinced, cannot be formulated in this case on the basis of spiritual "data," but only on the basis of economic facts over which few people, even in Russia, have a sufficiently broad grasp. Moscow, as it appears at the present, reveals a full range of possibilities in schematic form: above all, the possibility that the Revolution might fail or succeed. In either case, something unforeseeable will result and its picture will be far different from any programmatic sketch one

---

21.   Letter is from the Martin Buber collection, Jewish National Library, Hebrew University of Jerusalem. First printed in Walter Benjamin, *Briefe*, Theodor Adorno and Gershom Scholem, eds., Frankfurt, Suhrkamp, 1966, pp. 442–443.
22.   Joseph Wittig (1879–1949) was an editor of *Die Kreatur* from 1926–1928.

might draw of the future. The outlines of this are at present brutally and distinctly visible among the people and their environment.

That's it for today. Wishing you the best, I remain

Yours truly,
Walter Benjamin

[preface to a planned series for *Humanité*] [23]

I belong to that generation that is now between thirty and forty years old. The intelligentsia of this generation is far and away the last generation to have enjoyed a nonpolitical education. The war caught its most left-leaning elements in a position of more or less radical pacifism. The history of postwar Germany is partially the history of this originally leftist wing of the intelligentsia. One can be certain in asserting that the 1918 Revolution, which failed because of its petit-bourgeois parvenu spirit, did more to radicalize this generation than did the war itself. In Germany it is increasingly the case — and this is the most curious and important fact about this process — that the status of the unaffiliated writer is being put into question and one is gradually realizing that the writer (like the intellectual in the broadest sense of the term) consciously or unconsciously, willingly or unwillingly, works in the service of a class and receives his mandate from that class. Given the fact that it is ever more difficult for an intellectual to make a living, this particular realization has been accelerating of late. The political counter-pressure of the ruling class that has led during these past years to literary censorship and trials [crossed out: that evoke the days of the "Holy Alliance"] are part and parcel of the same process. Given these circumstances, the sympathy of the German intelligentsia for Russia is not merely abstract, but rather has to do with a concrete interest. It is curious to find out: how does the intelligentsia fare in a nation in which the proletariat is the employer? How does the proletariat define the conditions essential to its existence and what kind of environment will the intelligentsia find? What can it expect of a proletarian government? Given their sense of the evident crisis confronting the fate of the intelligentsia in bourgeois society, such writers as Toller, Holitscher,[24] and Leo Matthias,[25] such painters as Vogeler-Worpswede,[26] and such

23.   From the editorial apparatus to Benjamin's *Gesammelte Schriften*, vol. VI, Rolf Tiedemann and Hermann Schweppenhäuser, eds., Frankfurt, Suhrkamp, 1985, pp. 781–782.
24.   Arthur Holitscher (1869–1941), novelist and essayist. Benjamin had just read his *Der Fall Ravachol* (1925), according to an unpublished list he kept of books he read. In 1929 Benjamin reviewed *Es geschah in Moskau*, Berlin, S. Fischer, 1929 (*GS*, III, p. 166). Holitscher's writings include *Drei Monate in Sowjet-Russland* (1921) and *Das Theater im revolutionären Russland* (1924).
25.   Leo Matthias (1893–1970), translator, writer. Benjamin had recently read his *Genie und Wahnsinn in Russland* (1921). His other works include *Die Paritur der Welt* (1921) and *Ausflug nach Moskau* (1925).
26.   Heinrich Vogeler-Worpswede (1872–1942) published *Reise durch Russland* in 1925.

theater directors as Bernhard Reich have studied Russia and have reached out to their Russian colleagues. It is in the same sense that I found myself in a city where in my sheer capacity as a writer I enjoyed privileges of both a material and administrative sort. (I know of no other city except Moscow where the state would pay for a writer's room—after all, the hotels are all run by the Soviet.) The following pieces have been excerpted from a diary I kept there continuously over a period of eight weeks. I have attempted to convey an image of proletarian Moscow that one can come to know only when one has witnessed it under ice and snow, and above all I have tried to render the physiognomy of its workday and the new rhythm that informs both the life of the worker and that of the intellectual.

Paris
May 1, 1927

[excerpt from a letter by Benjamin]

Pardigon
June 5, 1927

My most esteemed Herr von Hofmannsthal,[27]
    I believe it has been almost a year since I last wrote you. In the meantime I have been in Russia, and if I let nothing transpire during my months in Moscow, it was because given the impact of my first impressions of this intense, foreign existence, I was unable to report anything. I had hoped to be able to include in my first letter to you my attempt at describing this stay. But although the galleys of the essay have been ready, it has not yet been published. In this essay I have tried to show those concrete manifestations of life that struck me the most deeply, and to show them just as they are and without any theoretical excursuses, if not without any private point of view of my own. Obviously, given my ignorance of the language I was not able to treat more than a rather narrow slice of life. But I have concentrated less on visual than on rhythmic experience, an experience in which an archaic Russian tempo blends into a whole with the new rhythms of the Revolution, an experience which, by Western standards, I discovered to be far more incommensurable than I had expected. — I had planned to undertake (somewhat incidentally) a literary project during my stay, but it fell through. The editors of the *Soviet Encyclopedia* intend to bring the work out in five stages, but very few competent researchers

27.   Hofmannsthal (1874–1929) recognized Benjamin's singularity very early and published his essay "Goethe's *Elective Affinities*" in the short-lived journal *Neue Deutsche Beiträge* in April 1924 and January 1925. Part of Benjamin's *Origin of German Tragic Drama* appeared in the same journal in August 1927. This letter is published in Benjamin, *Briefe*, pp. 443–446.

are available for the project and they are in no position to be able to carry out their gigantic enterprise. I myself was able to observe just how opportunistically they vacillated between their Marxist program of science and their desire to gain some sort of European prestige. But neither this private disappointment nor the difficulties and rigors of Moscow in the depth of winter were enough to lessen the powerful impression made by a city whose inhabitants are still reeling from the major battles in which everybody in some way or another was involved. I concluded my stay in Russia with a visit to Sergeiro-Lavra, the second-oldest monastery in the kingdom and the place of pilgrimage for all the boyars and czars. Rooms filled with bejeweled stoles, with an infinite number of illuminated gospels and prayer books, with manuscripts dating back to the Athos monks all the way through the seventeenth century, as well as countless icons from every period, clothed in gold, with the heads of the Madonnas gazing out of the gildings as if caught in Chinese neck-irons — I toured all this for more than an hour with the temperature twenty degrees below zero. It was like some giant freezer in which an ancient culture was being preserved under ice during the dog days of the Revolution. In the Berlin weeks that followed, I above all busied myself with selecting those things that seemed communicable from the detailed diary that I kept over the course of my journey, the first such diary I had written in fifteen years. When I got back to Germany the Proust had appeared [*Im Schatten der jungen Mädchen (A l'ombre des jeunes filles en fleurs)*] and I confirmed the fact that the publisher has sent you a copy in my absence. If you have a chance to glance at it, I hope you are not too unfavorably disposed toward it. It was well received by the critics. But what does that mean? I think I can honestly say that any translation that has been undertaken for the highest and most urgent reasons (for example, translations of the Bible) or for the sheer purpose of philological study, has something absurd about it. I would be happy if this were not too obtrusively evident in this case [. . .].

GARY SMITH

Benjamin's writings resist our impulse to taxonomize, and it would be reductive simply to classify the *Moscow Diary* among the autobiographical writings.[1] While the journal of his two months in Moscow is actually Benjamin's longest extant autobiographical document,[2] the text itself exceeds the conventions of the genre. As much an encyclopedic survey as a personal memoir, the diary form is better considered as a convenient rubric under which Benjamin might gather his impressions than as an accurate record of the quotidian. Benjamin was never able to sustain diary writing for long, and we may ascribe the length of the text to his commission to write an essay about Moscow for Martin Buber's *Die Kreatur*. Virtually every entry contains material which would later appear, transfigured, either in the essay "Moscow," or in one of the other essays on Soviet cultural life published after his return. Moreover, the journal is often characterized by that "absence of judgment" wherein "all factuality is already theory" which Benjamin had promised Buber. It is in this sense that we can speak of this as a "public" journal.

We read the *Moscow Diary* as if through a palimpsest: Benjamin's articles on the factions among Russian writers and on Meyerhold's *The Inspector General*, as well as more general discussions of Russian theater, film, poetry, and toys, were all fashioned from the motifs of the diary. Even the debut of Benjamin's writing for radio is to be located in the journal, which provided the material for a broadcast on young Russian poets.[3]

1. Walter Benjamin, *Moskauer Tagebuch*, ed. Gary Smith, pref. Gershom Scholem (Frankfurt, Suhrkamp, 1980). The diary and other autobiographical writings are published together with Benjamin's fragments in the most recent volume of his collected writings or *Gesammelte Schriften*, hereafter *GS*, VI, ed. Rolf Tiedemann and Hermann Schweppenhäuser. Frankfurt, Suhrkamp, 1985.
2. It is one of nineteen extant autobiographical texts, most of which, it should be noted, were written during trips.
3. Immediately related to his trip were "Disputation bei Meyerhold" (Feb. 11, 1927), "Rainer Maria Rilke und Franz Blei" (unpublished until *GS*, IV, 453–454), "Die politische Gruppierung der russischen Schriftsteller" (March 11, 1927), "Zur Lage der russischen Filmkunst" (March 11, 1927), "Erwiderung an Oscar A. H. Schmitz" (March 11, 1927), and "Russische Spielsachen"

The diary, then, will provide for the student of Benjamin a glimpse into his compositional practices: we can follow the evolution of his characteristic public style from the traces in his diary, and recognize the differences between the private Benjamin of this diary and the public Benjamin. But the journal is not only of biographical and literary interest. The text also engages the reader familiar with Soviet cultural politics at the earliest stages of Stalinization. During what was arguably the final winter of literary independence, Stalin was winning the struggle against Trotsky for succession to Lenin's place, and cultural policy was hardening. Benjamin draws for us not only the lineaments of Moscow in this winter, but also those of a number of leaders in the revolutionary arts. He provides details of the denouement of an independent sensibility in Soviet culture when, for example, he records meeting Lelevich, an important member of the literary opposition, the day before Lelevich is ushered eastward. He is also present, following the première of Meyerhold's *The Inspector General*, for the round-table debate which included Meyerhold, Mayakovsky, Lunacharsky, Bely, and many others.

The *Moscow Diary* gives us the vision and the voice of one who, still an outsider, is potentially a fellow-traveler. Indeed, in this respect, Benjamin is not unlike Bertolt Brecht or Karl Korsch, both Marxists of unusual pedigree — genealogically outsiders — with troubled relations to the Party. The text is studded with Benjamin's deliberations on whether or not to join the Communist Party; his futile efforts to secure publication prospects in the Soviet Union; his analysis of the precarious political situation around him, often through "factuality"; and the central autobiographical motif of the trip — his relationship to Asja Lacis and her lifelong companion, Bernhard Reich.

Just as Benjamin could identify different Cyrillic characters while being unable to discern their meanings, he could observe a performance or discussion but not understand its import. Often he attends the theater, only to chafe under his dependency on an interpreter. Nevertheless, he relies almost exclusively on Lacis and Reich, and not only for translation; it is they who decide where he is taken, whom he meets, and what he is shown. At some level, the Moscow Benjamin transcribes is that of his tour guide, Reich — Reich's handwriting is partially discernable through the palimpsest of the *Moscow Diary*.

(see this volume, pp. 123–124; January 10, 1930). Russian themes continued to traverse his publications through 1930. Cf. "Verein der Freunde des neuen Russland in Frankreich" (June 10, 1927), "Neue Dichtung in Russland" (1927), "Granowski erzahlt" (April 27, 1928), "Piscator und Russland" (May 27, 1929), "Wie ein russischer Theatererfolg aussieht" (January 17, 1930), "Russische Debatte auf Deutsch" (July 4, 1930), and reviews of books by Fyodor Gladkov, Ivan Schmelyow, Mikhail Zoshchenko (1928), Alexei A. Sidorov (1928), Arthur Holitscher (1929), and Nicolas von Arseniev (1929).

Benjamin's radio talk on March 23, 1927, on Sudwestdeutscher Rundfunk, Frankfurt, was in a series called "The Great Metropolises," and was preceded the week before by a "Moscow Letter" by Bernhard Reich.

Reich's independent connections are with the Austrians (Basseches and Russian diplomats once in Vienna such as Gnedin and Neiman) as well as with the
Soviet Encyclopedia project. Benjamin's disillusionment with Soviet cultural policy
is catalyzed by Reich, who introduces him to significant figures of the literary opposition, most importantly, the *On Guard*ist leadership (Lelevich, Bezymensky,
Lebedinsky). With Reich Benjamin discussed journalism and the respective
situations of the writer in the Soviet Union and in Germany. With Lacis in the
sanatorium, Reich shows Benjamin his (and her) Moscow. But the relationship
between the two men is anything but transparent: they share a passion for the
same woman, live under the strain of daily contact, and have competitive journalistic aims. From time to time Benjamin characterizes Reich in unflattering
ways. While perhaps the most vociferous argument of the trip arises over Benjamin's review of the Meyerhold production, only a few years earlier, in *Der
Querschnitt*, the two critics had jointly published an exchange of letters between
two fictional Elizabethan lords about *Hamlet*.[4]

A fragment formally, Benjamin's autobiographical text also offers a set of
thematic incompletions. About his position with respect to the Communist
Party, it remains inconclusive; about his relation to Asja Lacis, it is unre-
solved. Neither of these relationships is clarified, and Benjamin remains on the
outside, an outcast intruder into a relationship, out of place in postrevolutionary Russian life. And he is quicker to recognize and relinquish his naiveté
about his position in the Soviet Union than he is to acknowledge and confront
the hopelessness of his relationship with Lacis.

Among the many puzzles of this diary is that of the text's title. Benjamin
eradicated the now lost original name, replacing it with "Spanish Trip," probably for political reasons — to facilitate transporting the manuscript — though
other possible allusions are attractive to consider. Is he referring to a planned,
but unrealized trip to Spain with Lacis, for which this is a substitute? Or is it
that the Russian language sounds "Spanish" (the German equivalent of "It's
Greek to me" is "Es kommt mir Spanisch vor") to him, particularly since he made
so little progress in learning the language during his eight weeks in Moscow?

*

Those familiar with the lives of Bertolt Brecht and Walter Benjamin will
recognize the name Asja Lacis. It was she who first introduced them in May
1929, arranging a meeting that Benjamin had for several years requested. But
Brecht is present even here, three years earlier: Benjamin's report of his very
first meeting with Lacis in Moscow consists of, "I filled her in about Brecht."
Although he is not mentioned again in the diary, Brecht will soon become a

---

4.   Walter Benjamin and Bernhard Reich, "Revue oder Theater," *GS*, IV, pp. 796–802.

critical figure in Benjamin's life and writings, while Brecht's bonds with Lacis and Reich were never to be dissolved through separation, war, or internment.

For Brecht, as well as for Benjamin, Lacis was the earliest source of information about Soviet theater and cultural policy. She had studied in Moscow in the studio of Komissarzhevsky. Later, in Orel, she had used an obscure children's play by Meyerhold, *Alinea* (1919), in her successful children's theater.[5] Lacis and Reich first met Brecht while walking in Munich's English Garden in September 1923. Brecht had come to Munich to work on his adaptation (with Lion Feuchtwanger) of Marlowe's *Edward II* at the Kammerspiele, where Reich was stage director. Brecht hired Lacis as a director's assistant, and even gave her the small part of the young Edward. *Edward II*'s premiere was January 19, 1924. The play ran from January to March, and soon all of the principals had gone to Italy: Brecht, first to Capri and then to Positano (near the set designer Caspar Neher); Lacis and Reich (as of July), to Capri, where they met Marinetti and Maxim Gorky (in Sorrento). At the same time Benjamin himself was in Capri, where he spent time with Ernst Bloch.

It was, then, in Italy, that Benjamin and Lacis first met. In her autobiography Lacis describes her first encounter with Benjamin during a period when Reich had returned to his duties at the Munich Kammerspiele:

> Once I wanted to buy some almonds in a store. I didn't know what almonds were called in Italian, and the salesperson didn't understand what I wanted from him. Next to me was standing a man who said "Dear Lady, may I help you?" "Please," I said. I was given the almonds and went to the piazza with my package—the gentleman followed me and said: "May I accompany you and carry your packages?" I scrutinized him — and he continued: "Allow me to introduce myself — Dr. Walter Benjamin." I spoke my surname.
>
> My first impression — spectacles, which cast light forth like small headlights, thick dark hair, small nose, awkward hands—he dropped the packages. The sum being: a sober intellectual, one of the well-to-do. He accompanied me home, said good-bye, and asked if I would allow him to visit me again.

During September and October Benjamin and Lacis wrote the first of his *Denkbilder*, "Naples," published in 1925 in the *Frankfurter Zeitung*.[6] At this same time Brecht moved to Berlin to prepare *Man Is Man*, with Reich as one of the

5.   Benjamin wrote up a sort of pedagogical manifesto for this kind of theater in late 1928 or early 1929, probably at Lacis's request. See "Programm eines proletarischen Kindertheaters," *GS*, II/2, pp. 763–769.
6.   *GS*, IV, pp. 307–316.

"staff." During February and March of 1925 Brecht agreed to work with Reich on Dumas's *La dame aux camélias*, starring Elizabeth Bergner, by adapting Ferdinand Bruckner's translation and foregrounding the social aspects of the play. Brecht managed the reworking anonymously, and Bruckner was not told of the changes. Brecht added several parts to the play, including a small role for Lacis, and added a fifth act, which de-sentimentalized the ending. The production was a critical failure, Bruckner sued the theater, and Brecht, whose role now became public, was castigated along with Reich.

In November 1925 Benjamin unexpectedly visited Lacis in Riga, where she was directing an illegal agitprop theater. In addition to passages in her autobiography, we also know of the visit from a few revealing images in *One-Way Street*. In "Stereoscope," describing the paper rods in the Riga market, he writes, "Like being scolded by the most beloved voice—such are these rods" (p. 86); in "Ordnance," he remembers:

> I had arrived in Riga to visit a woman friend. Her house, the town, the language were unfamiliar to me. Nobody was expecting me, no one knew me. For two hours I walked the streets in solitude. Never again have I seen them so. From every gate a flame darted, each cornerstone sprayed sparks, and every streetcar came toward me like a fire engine. For she might have stepped out of the gateway, around a corner, been sitting in the streetcar. But of the two of us I had to be, at any price, the first to see the other. For had she touched me with the match of her eyes, I might have gone up like a magazine (pp. 68–69).

In *One-Way Street* Lacis often seems just around the page. These passages predate the Moscow diary, and the street, which he follows to Moscow, "is named Asja Lacis Street after the engineer who laid it through the author." In her autobiography *Revolutionär im Beruf*, Lacis claims to have provided the first impetus for Benjamin's turn towards Marxism. Benjamin seeks her approval of his plans, and even writes of a critique of psychology. "I once again realized just to what extent the possibility of tackling these subjects depends on my contact with her" (p. 10). Such observations, however, diminish in frequency as the diary proceeds. In fact, Lacis gives little evidence of providing substantive theoretical direction. Benjamin's most interesting discussions appear to be with Reich. While he is keen to present ideas to Lacis, the theme of their relationship, drawn as an erotic red thread throughout his journal, is one of obsession and denial.

It remains true, however, that Benjamin asserted Lacis's intellectual influence. As he wrote to Scholem at the end of 1924: ". . . the Communist signals . . . were first mark of a turn, which awoke the will in me, no longer to mask (as I had, primly) the actual and political moments in my thought, rather to develop them, and attempt to do this, radically."[7]

Benjamin was thirty-four when he traveled to Moscow. Reich had been working primarily as a theater critic for Russian newspapers, although he had made occasional contributions on Soviet culture to German papers such as the *Magdeburger Zeitung*. Shortly after Benjamin's return from Moscow, Reich also published several brief cultural notices in the *Literarische Welt*, where Benjamin was a regular contributor.[8] And in November 1928, it was Lacis and Reich who went to Berlin (Reich only for a visit), where Brecht was finishing *The Three-Penny Opera*. Lacis worked at the Soviet Embassy as a trade representative for Soviet films, arranging screenings which Brecht sometimes attended. She moved between two factions, the Brecht-Piscator group and the Alfred Kurella-Georg Lukács-Johannes Becher group, siding with the former. It was during this period, from 1928–1930, that Lacis lived with Benjamin for two months. When, through Lacis, Benjamin finally met Brecht in May 1929, Benjamin was almost thirty-seven and Brecht was thirty-one. Within a year Benjamin had produced a folder of diaries about his conversations with Brecht, and a historic, ten-year exchange was launched.[9] Benjamin and Brecht would collaborate in many ways, planning to "establish a very small reading circle, led by Brecht and myself, to destroy Heidegger," and to publish a journal, *Kritik und Krise*, at Rowohlt in the early 1930s; spending time together in Le Lavandou; and later, communing at Brecht's exile retreat in Svendborg.

At the same time as the friendship with Brecht began, Benjamin lost sight of, though not contact with, Lacis. He wrote to her in 1935 of his plans and sent a reprint of an essay from the *Zeitschrift für Sozialforschung*. She had returned to Moscow in 1930, where the next year she took part in Erwin Piscator's filming of Anna Seghers's *Aufstand der Fischer von S. Barbara* with John Heartfield and Lotte Lenya. In 1935 she published a book on German avant-garde theater, only to be interned the next year in Kazakhstan for over a decade. During these years Reich suffered repeated banishment and imprisonment. In September 1937 the contracts of all German émigrés were suddenly voided. Reich was

7.   Walter Benjamin, *Briefe*, G. Scholem and T. W. Adorno, eds., Frankfurt, Suhrkamp, 1966, p. 368.
8.   It is probable that Benjamin recommended Reich to Willy Haas, editor of the *Literarische Welt*. Three of Reich's contributions appeared in 1927, vol. 3: "Ein Sängerkrieg in Moskau" (no. 20), "Russische Literatur" (no. 35), and "Die russische Zeitung" (no. 35). The last contrasted the situations of Soviet and German journalists. The following year he published an interview with Eisenstein and reviewed a new Meyerhold production. In 1929 he published a letter about theater in Moscow.
9.   The most enlightening and accurate account of this friendship is Rolf Tiedemann's "Brecht oder die Kunst, in anderer Leute Kopfe zu denken," in R. T., *Dialektik im Stillstand* (Frankfurt, Suhrkamp, 1983), pp. 42–73. For Benjamin on Brecht, see Walter Benjamin, *Understanding Brecht* (London, New Left Books, 1973) and "A Radio Talk on Brecht," *New Left Review*, No. 123 (Sept.-Oct. 1980), pp. 92–96.

arrested during this year, released for a period at the end of December and again in May 1941, in order to meet with Brecht, who was traveling through the capital, and sometime thereafter banished from Moscow. Lacis and Reich reappeared together after the Stalin era, in both Moscow and Berlin, as Brecht's Moscow advisors at the Berliner Ensemble. After the war they wrote about and produced Brecht's works. Lacis was only allowed to work as a director after the Twentieth Party Congress in 1956, and she produced Brecht on the Latvian stage. Reich wrote a monograph in Russian on Brecht, published his politically silent autobiography, and compiled the first German-language edition of the theoretical writings of Meyerhold, Tairov, and Vakhtangov.[10]

*

A persistent theme throughout Benjamin's stay in Moscow is his inner conflict about membership in the Communist Party. Most commentators have underestimated the degree to which Benjamin was informed of developments within the German KPD and the consequent effect of his information on these deliberations. It is true that his early attraction to the Party was tied to his failure to secure an academic appointment and to his insecurity about his few journalistic staples, such as the *Literarische Welt*. Radicalized in the midst of his Frankfurt *Habilitation* attempt, Benjamin conceived an alternate plan. Only seven months before the Moscow trip Benjamin had characterized his flirtation with the Party as "experimental."

His decision was weighed on a scale of hope and disappointment, the outcome depending on the resistance to be met by his other publishing plans. If they failed, he planned immediately to join the KPD. He expressed this outright in a letter to Gershom Scholem: if the publication prospects were beached, then he would ''probably accelerate my involvement with Marxist politics—and with a view towards moving for a period to Moscow in the near future, for at least the moment—join the Party. I plan to take this step sooner or later in any case.''[11] Benjamin left for Moscow, however, with a stable number of associations and projects. He was a regular contributor to the Rowohlt journal *Literarische Welt*, a frequent reviewer for the *Frankfurter Zeitung*, and was translating Proust's *A la recherche du temps perdu* with Franz Hessel, first for the publishing house Die Schmiede, and later Piper Verlag.

Nevertheless, Benjamin is alert to the direction in which the German Communist Party is moving, and refers in a letter to the left-intellectual "opposition" within the KPD, one of whom, Gershom Scholem's brother, is called to Moscow while Benjamin is there and thrown out of the Party soon afterward. Benjamin's considerations about whether or not to join the Party are *not* simply

10. B. Reich, *Brecht* (Moscow, 1960); B. Reich, ed. *Theateroktober* (Leipzig, Reclam, 1967).
11. *Briefe*, pp. 381–382.

tied to journalistic-literary prospects, as has been suggested, but to more general, deep-seated misgivings about making an alliance with the Party during a period of pronounced anti-intellectualism. He felt both an "elective affinity" between himself and Werner Scholem, at the time a KPD member of the Reichstag, as well as "surprise about [his] touching with a radical Bolshevist theory. . . ."

Yet this does not mean that Benjamin's scruples about joining the Party were primarily ideological. In the diary he focuses on the security that membership would offer him — contacts and opportunities not available to an "outsider" of the left opposition. In fact, by the time of Benjamin's appearance in Moscow, the Party was increasingly impatient with its Russian fellow-travelers, though still solicitous of foreign ones, particularly through 1928, the celebration of the tenth anniversary of the Revolution. When Benjamin notes that strong political orientations are demanded of the Soviet intellectual, as opposed to the German fellow-traveler, for whom "only a vague and general political background suffices," he may very well be alluding to those writers in the Soviet Union who were not formally Party members, but who were sympathetically drawn to it. Such intellectuals, however, were then unevenly assimilated into Soviet cultural bureaucracy. Reich is thus fearful of what Benjamin might say in his interview, and Radek blasts Benjamin's Goethe article for a repetitious use of the term "class conflict." Ultimately, the decision not to join the Party was both a stand against Stalinism, which did not affect Benjamin's growing radicalism, and a signal of an upward turn in his journalistic career.

It must be remembered that Benjamin's acute psychological isolation in Moscow overshadows even his deliberations on the advantages and disadvantages of joining the Party. And this isolation was itself augmented by the anxiety engendered by the proletarianization of the cultural sphere. Years later, in his essay, "The Author as Producer," Benjamin faced this issue again: "No matter how revolutionary it may seem, [political commitment] will function in a counter-revolutionary way so long as the writer's solidarity with the proletariat is simply a matter of conviction and has not been experienced by him as producer."[12]

*

In the efflorescence of scholarship on Soviet theater, one production evoked by far the greatest response: Meyerhold's staging of Gogol's *The Inspector General*. Meyerhold restructured this Russian classic in a manner which would become standard for revolutionary Soviet theater. Incorporating dialogue from several different Gogol texts, the production was also revolutionary in its

12.   In *Reflections*, p. 226.

episodic structure and restricted performing space, creating the effect of a series of tableaux. The boundaries between performance and interpretation were broken down, and the theater remained open for hours after the final curtain, discussions about the evening's performances filling the auditorium. In her autobiography Lacis tells of Benjamin's spellbound reaction to the debate following *The Inspector General*, which he detailed in his report "Dispute at Meyerhold's":

> Thousands collected in the huge hall to discuss Meyerhold's staging of *The Inspector General.* They followed the controversy with every fiber, interrupting, applauding, shouting, whistling. The Russian speakers fascinated Benjamin; he thought they were born tribunes. Among others, Mayakovsky, Meyerhold, and Bely spoke. One wouldn't find this in Berlin.[13]

The significance of this event resurfaced when Benjamin later, in "What a Russian Theatrical Hit Looks Like," addressed the problem of Soviet theatrical criticism.[14] Three years after his return, he observed that "there are no prominent feuilleton critics in Russia, at least for the theater," because the overtness of the theater allows political tensions to be palpably manifested. The upshot according to Benjamin is that the only personalities influential as critics are political, public figures — for instance, Bukharin, reviewing the Meyerhold production for *Pravda*. He also cites a deeper reason for the critic's lack of influence, a reason reminiscent of the spectacle in Meyerhold's theater: the judgment of the individual critic is displaced by the "articulation of the initially eruptive, wordless mass verdict." But while Meyerhold's production was revolutionary to Soviet theatrical history, the agitation surrounding it adumbrated the end of the cultural-political "thaw" of the early 1920s in Soviet culture.

*

The diary first appeared in 1980 and is published in unabridged form. It was not published earlier for two reasons. First, the publishing house decided not to issue the diary during the lifetime of Asja Lacis. Secondly, the diary was scheduled for publication in the sixth volume of Benjamin's *Gesammelte Schriften*, which contains all of his extant autobiographical writings and fragments, other than those of the *Paris Arcades Project* (volume five).

The original manuscript is housed in the Theodor W. Adorno archive in Frankfurt-am-Main. The physical manuscript is a mere fifty-six pages long (21 cm by 13.4 cm), of which almost two pages are blank. Presumably Benjamin meant to use these pages to include a translation of his interview in the Moscow

13. "Disputation bei Meyerhold," *GS*, IV, pp. 481–483. Lacis, pp. 58–59.
14. "Wie ein Russischer Theatererfolg aussieht," *GS*, IV, pp. 561–563.

daily *Vecherniaia Moskva.* Differing ink colors indicate that Benjamin's last entries, those dated as of January 29, were made in Berlin. He left wide margins and relatively large amounts of space at the top and bottom of the manuscript on only the first few pages. Thereafter his strokes become increasingly compressed and miniature. After the eleventh page, he leaves no margin at all, and by the conclusion of the manuscript the number of words on each page has more than doubled from over 500 to more than 1100 words per page. Benjamin pencilled through forty-one passages in the journal, marking them for later plundering. Many of these are recognizable in his essay "Moscow," though greatly transfigured.

Since Benjamin knew no Russian, deciphering his inconsistent renderings of Russian names and other names became an often arduous exercise in free association. The original German edition reproduces Benjamin's own transliterations without revision; the present edition conventionalizes all spellings. This edition also supersedes the original edition in two respects. First, it incorporates textual corrections made by Rolf Tiedemann for volume six of Benjamin's collected works. Secondly, the editors of *October* have allowed me to revise and correct many of the notes, and a number of individuals not identified for the German edition have now been identified. I have deleted only those endnotes which compare passages in the journal to related passages in Benjamin's other writings. I originally intended these comparisons to draw attention to linguistic, stylistic, and thematic differences between the public and the private Benjamin, in a way not possible or appropriate in an English edition, given the paucity of Benjamin's works translated into English. The *Moscow Diary* is complemented by a number of letters, some of which were unknown six years ago.

I am greatly indebted to Gershom Scholem, Rolf Tiedemann, Siegfried Unseld, and Winfried Menninghaus. Professor Scholem spent many hours reviewing each sentence of the transcription together with the editor in Jerusalem and Frankfurt. Rolf Tiedemann, whose Benjamin and Adorno editions are models of editorial excellence, allowed me to use his own draft transcription of the diary, which immeasurably improved the final transcription. The publisher Siegfried Unseld of Suhrkamp Verlag generously gave me the unusual opportunity to edit this manuscript while still a student. He provided exceptional in-house facilities, and sent me to Jerusalem to review an advanced version of the manuscript with Professor Scholem. Winfried Menninghaus, while an editor at Suhrkamp, reviewed each note to the original edition with the editor and made many valuable suggestions. Finally, the German Academic Exchange Service (DAAD) generously supported me for a two-year period, during which all of the work on this manuscript was executed.

The English edition of the diary owes many a debt to Anne Janowitz, Richard Sieburth, and Joan Copjec, Annette Michelson, Douglas Crimp, and Christopher Phillips of *October.*

Index